Beyond Analytics: Unlocking the Hidden Power of Competitive Ad Intelligence

Prologue

In today's digital advertising competitive landscape, I opt to delve into the fascinating world of beyond analytics: unlocking the hidden power of competitive ad intelligence and explore the immense potential that lies beyond traditional analytics. In an era where businesses are constantly striving for an edge, understanding the dynamics of this hidden power can be the game-changer the digital advertising eco-system is searching for. Join me as I uncover the secrets of unlocking the hidden power of competitive ad intelligence, beyond analytics and discover how it can revolutionize advertising strategies. The focus of this book covers Competitive Ad Intelligence Overview, traditional ad analytics, Market Dynamics, Consumer Behavior Analysis, Data-driven Decision Making, Adapting to Platform Changes and Cross-Channel Strategies.

Competitive Ad Intelligence Overview
Understanding the competitive landscape is crucial in the digital advertising space. Competitive ad intelligence involves gathering and analyzing data related to the advertising strategies of the competitors. This includes monitoring and analyzing their ad creatives, placement strategies, targeting parameters, and overall campaign performance and Innovation of ad formats.

Traditional Ad Analytics
Ad analytics is the systematic evaluation of advertising campaigns to measure their effectiveness and optimize performance. This is done through the analysis of various metrics such as click-through rates, conversion rates, impressions, and engagement, that allows advertisers gain valuable insights into the impact of their ads. These analytics help advertisers understand audience behavior, identify successful strategies, and make data-driven decisions to improve ROI.

Market Dynamics
The digital advertising landscape is dynamic and influenced by various factors, including technological advancements, changes in consumer behavior, and market trends. Staying ahead requires continuous monitoring of these dynamics to adapt strategies accordingly. This involves shifts in platform popularity, changes in ad formats, or emerging technologies like augmented reality or interactive content.

Consumer Behavior Analysis: Successful advertisers pay close attention to consumer behavior. This involves understanding how target audiences interact with content, respond to different ad formats, and make purchasing decisions. Beyond traditional analytics, advertisers might leverage advanced tools like sentiment analysis and predictive modeling to gain deeper insights into consumer preferences.

Innovation in Ad Formats: Advertisers are always on the lookout for innovative ways to capture the audience's attention. This could involve experimenting with new ad formats, such as interactive ads, interstitial Ads, shoppable content, or immersive experiences. Understanding what works for your industry and audience is essential for staying ahead.

Data-driven Decision Making: Beyond basic analytics, advertisers are increasingly relying on advanced data analytics and artificial intelligence to inform their decisions. This includes predictive analytics for forecasting campaign outcomes, using machine learning algorithms to optimize targeting, and leveraging big data to gain comprehensive insights.

Adapting to Platform Changes: Platforms like Google, Facebook, Instagram, X/twitter and others frequently update their algorithms and ad policies. Staying ahead requires a proactive approach to understanding these changes and adapting strategies accordingly. This could involve adjusting targeting parameters, optimizing ad creatives, or exploring new platform features.

Cross-Channel Strategies: Advertisers often find success by diversifying their advertising efforts across multiple channels. This might include a combination of social media advertising, search engine marketing (SEO & PPC), display advertising, and more. Understanding how to integrate and optimize campaigns across these channels is a key aspect of competitive ad intelligence.

Summary
Staying ahead in the competitive landscape of digital advertising involves a multifaceted approach that combines market awareness, consumer insights, and the strategic use of data and technology. Advertisers who unlock the hidden power of competitive ad intelligence are better positioned to adapt to changing dynamics and gain a competitive edge in the ever-evolving digital advertising space.

An Inspiring Story to Become A Competitive Ad Intelligence Expert, Beyond Analytics

Once upon a time in the fast-paced world of digital advertising, there lived a young and ambitious individual named Alexido. Alexido was fascinated by the ever-evolving landscape of online advertising and the power it held in connecting businesses with their target audiences. However, Alexido felt a burning desire to understand the intricacies of the industry at a deeper level, particularly the secrets hidden within the realm of competitive ad intelligence.

With a thirst for knowledge and a determination to excel, Alexido embarked on a journey to become a competitive ad intelligence expert, beyond analytics. The path was challenging, filled with unknown territories and complexities that seemed daunting at first. But Alexido was not one to back down from a challenge; instead, each obstacle became an opportunity for growth.

The first step on this transformative journey was to immerse himself in the world of digital advertising. Alexido devoured books, attended webinars, and engaged in online fora to grasp the fundamental concepts of digital advertising. This foundation served as the bedrock upon which Alexido would build a formidable expertise.

The next phase involved gaining hands-on experience by working on real-world projects. Alexido sought internships and collaborated with industry experts, absorbing insights and techniques like a sponge. The process was intense, demanding countless hours of analysis and experimentation. Yet, each campaign analyzed and every competitor dissected brought Alexido closer to mastery.

In the pursuit of excellence, Alexido recognized the importance of staying abreast of industry trends and technological advancements. Continuous learning became a way of life, and attending conferences, workshops, and networking events became routine. This commitment to staying ahead of the curve propelled Alexido to the forefront of the competitive ad intelligence field, beyond analytics.

As time passed, Alexido's reputation as a competitive ad intelligence expert, beyond analytics grew. Companies sought Alexido's expertise to gain a competitive edge in the fierce digital advertising battleground. Alexido's insights became invaluable, and success stories of campaigns propelled by strategic intelligence spread far and wide.

However, Alexido never forgot the initial struggles and the determination that fueled this incredible journey. In a gesture of gratitude to the community, Alexido began mentoring aspiring ad intelligence enthusiasts, sharing knowledge and empowering the next generation of experts.

In the end, Alexido's story serves as a beacon of inspiration for anyone aspiring to become a competitive ad intelligence expert, beyond analytics. Through unwavering determination, continuous learning, and a commitment to excellence, Alexido not only conquered the complexities of the digital advertising landscape but also paved the way for others to follow suit. And so, the fame of Alexido, a competitive ad intelligence expert, beyond analytics continues to inspire aspiring marketers to this day. Do you want to become the next Alexido? Read on and use the next page's poetical compass as a guide to achieve your dream.

Poetical Compass: Becoming the Next Alexido - A Competitive Ad Intelligence Expert, Beyond Analytics

In the realm of pixels and data's dance,
A compass of poesy, a poetic trance.
Becoming the next Alexido's call,
In the world of ads, where titans fall.

Navigate the seas of keywords bright,
Where insights gleam in the digital night.
Ad intelligence, a mystic art,
In the symphony of algorithms, play your part.

Chart the courses through competitive waves,
Where creativity and strategy behave.
Alexido's legacy, a beacon afar,
Illuminate the path, like a guiding star.

In the arena of pixels and ad campaigns,
Craft your narrative, break the chains.
The landscape shifts, a dynamic play,
Stay agile, adapt, and own the day.

The keywords whisper, secrets unfold,
In the labyrinth of searches, stories untold.
Decode the language of clicks and views,
In the kaleidoscope of data, find your clues.

Analytics, a canvas where patterns paint,
A masterpiece emerges, restraint and faint.
Becoming the next Alexido, a quest,
In the algorithms' embrace, be the best.

Compete not just with numbers and codes,
But with the symphony that creativity bodes.
In the heart of data, find the emotion,
Crafting campaigns, a poetic devotion.

Let your strategies bloom like spring,
In the garden of ads, let success sing.
Alexido's footsteps echo strong,
A competitive spirit, a lifelong song.

So, poetical compass, navigate with grace,
In the vast ocean of pixels, find your space.
Becoming the next Alexido, a journey profound,
In the world of ad intelligence, let your echo resound.

Preface

Welcome to "Beyond Analytics: Unlocking the Hidden Power of Competitive Ad Intelligence." In an era where digital landscapes evolve at an unprecedented pace, businesses navigate through a maze of information, seeking the most effective ways to connect with their audiences. The heartbeat of this transformation lies in the realm of advertising, where strategic decisions are powered by insights derived from analytics. However, the landscape has shifted beyond traditional analytics, urging us to explore the uncharted territory that focusses on Competitive Ad Intelligence.

This book is a comprehensive exploration of the multifaceted structures that make up the contemporary advertising ecosystem. The journey begins with a meticulous overview of Competitive Ad Intelligence, a discipline that transcends conventional analytics by delving into the strategies and tactics employed by competitors. In an age where information is not only power but a strategic asset, understanding how your rivals navigate the advertising space becomes paramount.

The chapters that follow provide in-depth insights into various aspects of Competitive Ad Intelligence. I unravel the intricacies of traditional ad analytics, offering a foundation upon which I build the narrative of the book. Moving forward, I delve into the dynamic forces that shape the advertising market, emphasizing the need for businesses to adapt and innovate continuously. Consumer Behavior Analysis emerges as a key pillar, exploring the psychology and patterns that govern the choices consumers make in response to advertising stimuli.

The heart of the book beats in rhythm with the pulse of data-driven decision making. I explore how businesses harness the power of data to make informed, strategic choices that propel them ahead in the fiercely competitive advertising landscape. The narrative extends to the challenges posed by the ever-evolving platforms, urging readers to stay vigilant and adapt to changes in order to stay ahead of the curve.

Finally, I conclude my journey with a discussion on Cross-Channel Strategies, recognizing that successful advertising campaigns traverse multiple platforms seamlessly. Navigating the crossroads of various channels requires a nuanced understanding of each, and this section provides practical insights to help businesses craft cohesive, effective strategies.

"Beyond Analytics: Unlocking the Hidden Power of Competitive Ad Intelligence" is more than just a guide; it is a roadmap for businesses looking to not only survive but thrive in the dynamic world of advertising. Whether you're a seasoned marketing professional, a business owner, or a curious mind eager to understand the forces driving the advertising industry, this book is your companion on the journey to unlocking the hidden power of Competitive Ad Intelligence. The exploration begins.

Brief Contents

Section 1: Introducing Beyond Analytics: Unlocking the Hidden Power of Competitive Ad Intelligence 18

Section 2: Traditional Digital Ad Analytics 33

Section 3: Market Dynamics 29

Section 4: Consumer Behavior Analysis 32

Section 5: Data-Driven Decision Making 36

Section 6: Competitive Ad Intelligence: A New Paradigm 40

Section 7: Tools and Technology for Competitive Ad Intelligence 54

Section 8: Adapting to Platform Changes 59

Section 9: Leveraging Emerging Technologies 63

Section 10: Ethical Considerations in Competitive Ad Intelligence 68

Section 11: Strategic Implementation of Competitive Ad Intelligence 72

Section 12: Case Studies of Successful Implementation of Competitive Ad intelligence 75

Section 13: Recap of Key Concepts in Competitive Ad Intelligence 76

Section 14: Glossary of Terms 80

Section 15: Resources 82

Section 16: About the Author 84

Overview

Section 1: Introducing Beyond Analytics: Unlocking the Hidden Power of Competitive Ad Intelligence 18

A. The Evolution of Digital Ad Analytics
- Tracing the historical development of ad analytics and its transformative journey.

B. The Need for a Comprehensive Approach
- Addressing the limitations of traditional ad analytics and introducing the necessity of a broader perspective.

C. Overview of Key Concepts
- Providing a foundational understanding of key concepts that lay the groundwork for competitive ad intelligence.

Section 2: Traditional Digital Ad Analytics 22

A. Historical Perspectives
- Examining the roots and evolution of traditional ad analytics.

B. Role of Analytics in Ad Campaigns
- Assessing the integral role analytics plays in shaping effective ad campaigns.

C. Issues with Traditional Analytics – Challenges and Limitations
- Identifying the shortcomings of conventional approaches and the challenges they pose.

D. Need for a More Comprehensive Approach Beyond Analytics
- Exploring the gaps in traditional methods and making the case for a more comprehensive strategy.

E. Commonly Used Analytics Tools and Metrics
- Surveying the landscape of commonly employed tools and metrics in the field.

F. Case Studies
- Examining real-world examples to illustrate successes and failures in traditional ad analytics.

Section 3: Market Dynamics: Understanding the Competitive Landscape through Ad Intelligence 29

A. Understanding the Competitive Landscape
- Providing insights into the dynamics of the competitive advertising environment.

B. Industry Trends and Innovations
- Analyzing current trends and innovative practices shaping the advertising industry.

C. Impact on Advertising Strategies
- Investigating how market dynamics influence the formulation of effective advertising strategies.

Section 4: Consumer Behavior Analysis 32

A. The Psychology of Consumer Decision making
- Delving into the psychological aspects that drive consumer decision-making.

B. Utilizing Behavioral Data
- Exploring the effective use of behavioral data to understand and predict consumer actions.

C. Personalization and Targeting Strategies
- Discussing strategies for personalization and targeted advertising based on consumer behavior analysis.

Section 5: Data-Driven Decision Making 36

A. Leveraging Big Data for Ad Insights
- Unpacking the potential of big data in extracting valuable insights for advertising.

B. Implementing Advanced Analytics Tools
- Exploring the integration of cutting-edge analytics tools to enhance decision-making.

C. Real-time Decision-Making in Advertising
- Examining the role of real-time data in shaping advertising strategies.

Section 6: Competitive Ad Intelligence: A New Paradigm 40

A. Defining Competitive Ad Intelligence

Understanding Competitors Beyond Basic Analytics: This section explores the depth of competitive analysis, going beyond surface-level metrics to unveil the strategies, strengths, and weaknesses of competitors.

Incorporating Competitive Intelligence into Advertising Strategy: Readers discover how to integrate competitive insights seamlessly into their advertising strategies, creating campaigns that stand out in the market.

B. Components of Competitive Ad Intelligence

Ad Creatives Analysis
Uncovering Successful Creative Strategies: Dive into the examination of successful creative approaches, unveiling the secrets behind compelling advertisements.

Analyzing Design Elements, Messaging, and Calls-to-Action: Learn to dissect the intricacies of design, messaging, and calls-to-action to create more impactful and engaging ad creatives.

Target Audience Insights
Identifying Competitor Target Demographics: Understand the demographics targeted by competitors, allowing for more precise audience targeting.

Leveraging Audience Data for Better Targeting: Explore the effective use of audience data to refine targeting strategies and reach the most receptive audience.

Ad Placement and Channel Strategy
Analyzing Where Competitors Are Advertising: Gain insights into competitors' ad placements, identifying the most lucrative channels for reaching the target audience.

Optimizing Ad Placement for Maximum Impact: Learn strategies to optimize ad placement for maximum visibility and impact.

Section 7: Tools and Technologies for Competitive Ad Intelligence 54

A. Advanced Analytics Platforms
Overview of Cutting-edge Analytics Tools: Explore the latest and most powerful analytics tools available, providing a comprehensive overview of their capabilities.

Integration of AI and Machine Learning in Competitive Ad Intelligence
Understand how artificial intelligence and machine learning are transforming competitive ad intelligence, enabling marketers to stay ahead of the curve.

Section 8: Adapting to Platform Changes 59

A. The Dynamic Nature of Advertising Platforms: Uncover the ever-changing dynamics of advertising platforms and the impact on advertising strategies.

B. Strategies for Adapting to Algorithm Updates: Explore effective approaches to staying ahead of algorithmic changes to maximize ad campaign success.

C. Case Studies of Successful Adaptation: Real-world examples showcasing successful adaptation strategies in response to platform changes.

Section 9: Leveraging Emerging Technologies 63

A. AI and Machine Learning in Advertising: Delve into the integration of AI and machine learning in advertising for more intelligent and effective campaigns.

B. Blockchain and its Impact on Ad Transparency: Understand the role of blockchain in ensuring transparency and accountability in advertising.

C. Virtual and Augmented Reality in Ad Campaigns: Explore the potential of virtual and augmented reality in creating immersive and engaging ad experiences.

Section 10: Ethical Considerations in Competitive Ad Intelligence 68

A. Privacy Concerns: Address the ethical implications surrounding privacy concerns in the collection and use of competitive ad intelligence.

B. Responsible Data Usage: Explore principles for responsible and ethical data usage in advertising.

C. Regulatory Compliance: Navigate the evolving regulatory landscape and ensure compliance in competitive ad intelligence practices.

Section 11: Strategic Implementation of Competitive Ad Intelligence 72

A. Current Analytics Practices

B. Strategic Option

C. Integrating Competitive Intelligence into Existing Workflows

Section 12: Case Studies of Successful Implementation of Competitive Ad Intelligence 75

Case Study 1

Case Study 2

Section 13: Future Trends in Competitive Ad Intelligence 76

A. Shifting Consumer Behavior

B. Moving Beyond Traditional Analytics

C. Ongoing Learning in Staying Ahead

Section 14: Recap of Key Concepts in Competitive Ad Intelligence 80

A. Glossary of Terms

Section 15: Resources 82

A. Performance Index

Section 16: About the Author 84

Table of Contents

Section: 1. Introducing Beyond Analytics: Unlocking the Hidden Power of Competitive Ad Intelligence 18

A. The Evolution of Ad Analytics 19

B. The Need for a Comprehensive Approach 20

C. Overview of Key Concepts 21

Section: 2. Traditional Ad Analytics 22

A. Historical Perspectives 23

B. Role of Analytics in Ad Campaigns 24

C. Issues with Traditional Analytics – Challenges and Limitations 25

D. Need for a More Comprehensive Approach Beyond Analytics 26

E. Commonly Used Analytics Tools and Metrics 27

F. Case Studies 28

Section: 3. Market Dynamics - Understanding the Competitive Landscape through Ad Intelligence 29

A. Industry Trends and Innovations 30

B. Impact on Advertising Strategies 31

Section: 4. Consumer Behavior Analysis 32

A. The Psychology of Consumer Decision-making 33

B. Utilizing Behavioral Data 34

C. Personalization and Targeting Strategies 35

Section: 5. Data-Driven Decision Making: How Competitive Ad Intelligence Transforms Strategy 36

A. Leveraging Big Data for Ad Insights 37

B. Implementing Advanced Analytics Tools 38

C. Real-time Decision-Making in Advertising 39

Section: 6. Competitive Ad Intelligence: A New Paradigm 40

A. Defining Competitive Ad Intelligence 41

1. Understanding Competitors Beyond Analytics 42

2. Incorporating Competitive Intelligence into Advertising Strategy 43

B. Components of Competitive Ad Intelligence 44

1. Ad Creatives Analysis 45

a. Uncovering Successful Creative Strategies 46

b. Analyzing Design Elements, Messaging, and Calls-to-action 47

2. Target Audience Insights 48

a. Identifying Competitor Target Demographics 49

b. Leveraging Audience Data for Better Targeting 50

3. Ad Placement and Channel Strategy 51

a. Analyzing Where Competitors Are Advertising 52

b. Optimizing Ad Placement for Maximum Impact 53

Section: 7. Tools and Technologies for Competitive Ad Intelligence 54

A. Advanced Analytics Platforms 55

1. Overview of Cutting-edge Analytics Tools 56

2. Integration of AI and Machine Learning in Competitive Ad Intelligence 57

3. The Role of Predictive Modelling in Competitive Ad Intelligence 58

Section: 8. Adapting to Platform Changes 59

A. The Dynamic Nature of Advertising Platforms 60

B. Strategies for Adapting to Algorithm Updates 61

C. Case Studies of Successful Adaptation 62

Section: 9. Leveraging Emerging Technologies of Blockchain and, Virtual and Augmented Reality 63

A. Blockchain Technology 64

B. The Impact of Blockchain on Competitive Ad Intelligence 65

C. Virtual and Augmented Reality Technology 66

D. The Impact of Virtual and Augmented Reality on Competitive Ad Intelligence 67

Section: 10. Ethical Considerations in Competitive Ad Intelligence 68

A. Privacy Concerns 69

B. Responsible Data Usage 70

C. Regulatory Compliance 71

Section: 11. Strategic Implementation of Competitive Ad Intelligence 72

A. Strategic Option 73

B. Integrating Competitive Ad Intelligence into Existing Workflows 74

Section: 12. Case Studies of Successful Implementation of Competitive Ad Intelligence 75

1. Case Study 1

2. Case Study 2

Section: 13. The Future Trends in Competitive Ad Intelligence 76

A. Shifting Consumer Behaviors 77

B. Moving Beyond Traditional Analytics 78

C. Ongoing Learning in Staying Ahead 79

Section: 14. Recap of Key Concepts in Competitive Ad Intelligence 80

A.   Glossary of Terms 81

Section: 15. Resources 82

A. Performance Index 83

Section 16. About the Author 84

Section 1

Introducing Beyond Analytics: Unlocking the Hidden Power of Competitive Ad Intelligence

In the digital advertising landscape, understanding your competition is key to staying ahead in the game. Competitive ad intelligence is a powerful tool that helps you unlock the hidden potential of your advertising strategy. In this section, I will introduce you to Beyond Analytics, a cutting-edge platform that offers advanced competitive ad intelligence solutions.

Understanding what your competitors are doing in their brand advertising provides valuable insights into their strategies and helps you make informed decisions for your own campaigns. Beyond Analytics goes beyond traditional analytics tools by offering a comprehensive view of your competitors' ad campaigns, including their ad creatives, targeting strategies, and performance metrics.

With Beyond Analytics, you track your competitors' ad campaigns across multiple channels and platforms, giving you a holistic view of their advertising efforts. By analyzing the data, you can identify trends, uncover new opportunities, and optimize your own campaigns for better results.

Beyond Analytics also offers advanced features such as real-time monitoring, competitive benchmarking, and predictive analytics, allowing you to stay one step ahead of the competition. Whether you are a small business looking to increase brand awareness or a large corporation trying to dominate your industry, competitive ad intelligence gives you the edge you need to succeed.

Summary

Beyond Analytics is a game-changing approach that can help you unlock the hidden power of competitive ad intelligence. By leveraging this tool, you can gain valuable insights into your competitors' strategies and make data-driven decisions to improve your own advertising efforts. Stay ahead of the competition with Beyond Analytics and take your digital advertising to the next level.

A. The Evolution of Digital Ad Analytics

In the ever-evolving world of advertising, keeping up with the latest trends and technologies is crucial for businesses looking to stay ahead of the competition. One area that has seen significant advancements in recent years is digital ad analytics. By utilizing competitive ad intelligence, companies gain valuable insights into their competitors' advertising strategies and make more informed decisions about their own campaigns.

The evolution of digital ad analytics is traced back to the early days of online advertising when businesses relied on simple metrics like click-through and conversion rates to measure the success of their campaigns. However, as the digital landscape becomes more complex, so too have the tools available for analyzing ad performance. Today, competitive ad intelligence platforms offer a wealth of data and insights that go far beyond traditional metrics, allowing businesses to gain a deeper understanding of their competitors' strategies and make more strategic decisions about their own advertising efforts.

One of the key benefits of using competitive ad intelligence is the ability to track and analyze the performance of your competitors' ads in real-time. By monitoring the ads that are resonating with your target audience and identifying the strategies that are driving the most engagement, you gain a competitive edge and optimize your own campaigns for maximum impact. Additionally, by analyzing the keywords and targeting strategies that your competitors are using, you identify new opportunities for reaching your audience and refining your messaging.

Summary

Overall, the evolution of digital ad analytics has revolutionized the way businesses approach online advertising, allowing them to gain deeper insights into their competitors' strategies and make more informed decisions about their own campaigns. By leveraging competitive ad intelligence, businesses stay ahead of the curve and drive better results for their advertising efforts.

B. The Need for a Comprehensive Approach

In today's fast-paced and ever-evolving digital landscape, businesses are constantly seeking ways to stay ahead of the competition. One key strategy that has become increasingly important is competitive ad intelligence. By analyzing the advertising strategies of competitors, businesses gain valuable insights into market trends, consumer behavior, and potential opportunities for growth.

However, simply monitoring the ads of competitors is not enough. To truly succeed in today's competitive market, businesses need to take a comprehensive approach to competitive ad intelligence. This means not only tracking and analyzing the ads of competitors, but also taking into account other factors such as target audience, messaging, and overall marketing strategy.

One of the key benefits of taking a comprehensive approach to competitive ad intelligence is the ability to identify gaps and opportunities in the market. By analyzing not only the ads themselves, but also the overall marketing strategy of competitors, businesses gain a more holistic view of the competitive landscape and better understand of where to differentiate themselves and capitalize on untapped markets.

Another important aspect of a comprehensive approach to competitive ad intelligence is the ability to adapt and evolve in real-time. By constantly monitoring and analyzing the advertising strategies of competitors, businesses quickly identify and respond to changes in the market, ensuring that they stay ahead of the competition and continue to drive growth.

Summary

The need for a comprehensive approach to competitive ad intelligence has never been greater. By taking a holistic view of the competitive landscape and leveraging insights from competitive ad intelligence, businesses gain a competitive edge, identify new opportunities for growth, and ultimately drive success in today's fast-paced digital market.

C. Overview of Key Concepts

Competitive ad intelligence is a crucial tool for staying ahead of the competition. By analyzing the advertising strategies of your competitors, you gain valuable insights into what is working and what isn't in your industry. In this segment, I will provide an overview of key concepts related to competitive ad intelligence.

1. Competitive Analysis: One of the primary goals of competitive ad intelligence is to conduct a thorough analysis of your competitors' advertising strategies. This involves identifying their target audience, copy decision, ad creatives, ad placements, and overall approach to digital advertising.

2. Ad Monitoring: Monitoring your competitors' ads is essential for staying informed about the latest trends in your industry. By keeping a close eye on their campaigns, you identify opportunities to improve your own advertising efforts and stay one step ahead of the competition.

3. Keyword Research: Keywords are the foundation of any successful digital advertising campaign. By conducting thorough keyword research, you identify the most relevant and high-performing keywords in your industry and incorporate them into your own ad campaigns.

4. Ad Performance Metrics: Tracking the performance of your competitors' ads is key to understanding what resonates with their target audience. By analyzing metrics such as click-through rates, conversion rates, and engagement levels, you gain valuable insights into the effectiveness of their advertising strategies.

5. Competitive Benchmarking: Benchmarking your own ad performance against that of your competitors is a crucial step in improving your digital advertising efforts. By comparing key metrics such as ad spend, click-through rates, and conversion rates, you identify areas where you are underperforming and make the necessary adjustments to boost your results.

Summary

Competitive ad intelligence is a powerful tool for gaining a competitive edge in the digital advertising landscape. By analyzing your competitors' advertising strategies, monitoring their ads, conducting keyword research, tracking ad performance metrics, and benchmarking your own performance, you stay ahead of the competition and drive success for your business.

Section: 2

Traditional Digital Ad Analytics

In the world of digital advertising, keeping tabs on your competitors is crucial for staying ahead in the game. Traditional digital ad analytics, combined with competitive ad intelligence, provide valuable insights into what your competitors are doing and how you can leverage that information to improve your own advertising strategies.

Competitive ad intelligence involves monitoring and analyzing the advertising activities of your competitors. This includes tracking their ad creatives, ad placements, copy decision, and targeting strategies across various digital platforms. By understanding what is working for your competitors, you identify opportunities to differentiate your own ads and capture a larger share of the market.

One key aspect of traditional digital ad analytics is tracking key performance indicators (KPIs) such as click-through rates, conversion rates, and return on ad spend (ROADS). By comparing your performance metrics to those of your competitors, you identify areas where you are falling short and make adjustments to improve your results.

Another important component of competitive ad intelligence is analyzing the creative and copy decision strategies of your competitors. By studying their ad copy, images, and calls to action, you gain insights into what resonates with your target audience and tailor your own ads accordingly.

In addition to monitoring your competitors, traditional digital ad analytics also help you track industry trends and benchmark your performance against industry standards. By staying informed about the latest developments in digital advertising, you ensure that your campaigns remain relevant and effective.

Overall, combining traditional digital ad analytics with competitive ad intelligence provide a comprehensive view of the competitive landscape and help you make informed decisions to drive your advertising success. By staying one step ahead of your competitors, you position your brand for long-term growth and success in the digital advertising space.

A. Historical Perspectives

In this section, I will delve into the historical perspectives of competitive ad intelligence. Understanding the evolution of competitive ad intelligence provide valuable insights into how businesses have adapted their advertising strategies over time.

Competitive ad intelligence has been a crucial aspect of advertising for decades, dating back to the early days of print advertising. Companies would closely monitor their competitors' ads in newspapers and magazines to gain insights into their copy decision and positioning.

As technology advanced, competitive ad intelligence evolved to include monitoring television commercials and radio ads. This allowed businesses to stay ahead of the competition by analyzing the effectiveness of different advertising campaigns.

In the digital age, competitive ad intelligence has taken on a whole new level of importance. With the rise of online advertising platforms such as Google AdWords and Facebook Ads, businesses now have access to a wealth of data on their competitors' digital advertising strategies.

By analyzing metrics such as ad placement, targeting, and copy decision, businesses gain valuable insights into what is working for their competitors and adjust their own advertising strategies accordingly.

Summary

Understanding the historical perspectives of competitive ad intelligence provide businesses with a deeper appreciation of the importance of staying ahead of the competition. By leveraging the latest tools and technologies, businesses gain a competitive edge in the ever-evolving world of advertising.

B. Role of Analytics in Digital Ad Campaigns

The role of analytics is crucial in ensuring the success of ad campaigns. By utilizing competitive ad intelligence, marketers gain valuable insights into their competitors' strategies and performance, allowing them to make data-driven decisions to optimize their own campaigns.

Competitive ad intelligence involves analyzing data on competitors' ad placements, ad creatives, targeting strategies, and performance metrics. By understanding what is working for their competitors, marketers identify opportunities to differentiate their own campaigns and gain a competitive edge.

One key aspect of competitive ad intelligence is monitoring ad performance metrics such as click-through rates, conversion rates, and return on ad spend (ROADS). By tracking these metrics, marketers identify which ads are most effective in driving desired outcomes and allocate budget towards high-performing campaigns.

Another important use of competitive ad intelligence is in identifying new trends and emerging competitors in the digital advertising landscape. By keeping a close eye on competitors' ad placements and creative strategies, marketers stay ahead of the curve and adapt their own campaigns to capitalize on new opportunities.

Overall, the role of analytics in digital ad campaigns, particularly when utilizing competitive ad intelligence, is essential in driving success and staying competitive in today's fast-paced digital advertising landscape. By leveraging data-driven insights, marketers optimize their campaigns, maximize ROI, and achieve their advertising goals.

C. Issues with Traditional Analytics – Challenges and Limitations

Traditional analytics has long been the go-to method for businesses looking to gain insights into their competitors' strategies and performance. However, there are several issues and limitations associated with this approach that hinder a company's ability to stay ahead of the competition.

One of the main challenges with traditional analytics is the reliance on historical data. While the data provide valuable information about past trends and performance, it may not accurately reflect current market conditions or competitor activities. This leads to outdated or incomplete insights that do not accurately represent the competitive landscape.

Another limitation of traditional analytics is the lack of real-time data. In today's fast-paced business environment, companies need to be able to quickly adapt to changing market conditions and competitor strategies. Traditional analytics often rely on data that are days or even weeks old, making it difficult for businesses to make timely decisions.

Additionally, traditional analytics may not provide a comprehensive view of the competitive landscape. Many companies focus solely on their direct competitors, failing to consider the broader market dynamics that impact their business. This narrow focus leads to missed opportunities and a lack of strategic insight.

To overcome these challenges and limitations, businesses turn to competitive ad intelligence tools. These tools provide real-time data on competitors' advertising strategies, including ad placements, copy decision, and performance metrics. By leveraging this piece of information, businesses gain a more accurate and up-to-date view of the competitive landscape, allowing them to make more informed decisions and stay ahead of the competition.

Summary

While traditional analytics has long been a valuable tool for businesses, they are not without their limitations. By incorporating competitive ad intelligence tools into their analytics strategy, companies overcome these challenges and gain a more comprehensive and timely view of the competitive landscape.

D. Need for a More Comprehensive Approach Beyond Analytics

In today's highly competitive business landscape, having a strong understanding of your competitors' advertising strategies is crucial for staying ahead in the game. While analytics provides valuable insights into your own performance and audience behavior, a more comprehensive approach that encompasses competitive ad intelligence is needed to truly thrive in the market.

Competitive ad intelligence goes beyond just analyzing your own data and delves into the strategies and tactics being employed by your competitors. By monitoring their advertising campaigns, you gain valuable insights into their target audience, copy decision, and overall marketing strategy. This piece of information helps you identify gaps in the market, capitalize on emerging trends, and stay one step ahead of the competition.

In addition to providing a more holistic view of the market landscape, competitive ad intelligence also helps you make more informed decisions when it comes to your own advertising efforts. By understanding what is resonating with your competitors' audiences, you tailor your own messaging and creative to better appeal to your target demographic. This ultimately leads to more effective campaigns and better ROI on your marketing spend.

Overall, while analytics play a crucial role in understanding your own performance, a more comprehensive approach that includes competitive ad intelligence is essential for staying competitive in today's fast-paced business environment. By staying informed about your competitors' strategies and leveraging this piece of information to inform your own marketing efforts, you position yourself for success and drive growth in your business.

E. Commonly Used Analytics Tools and Metrics

When it comes to analyzing the performance of your online advertising campaigns, there are a variety of tools and metrics that help you gain valuable insights into how your ads are performing and how they stack up against your competitors. In this segment, I will explore some commonly used analytics tools and metrics, with a focus on competitive ad intelligence.

By using competitive ad intelligence tools, you track your competitors' ad placements, ad copy, targeting strategies, and more, giving you a competitive edge in the crowded online advertising space.

One of the most popular tools for competitive ad intelligence is Adbeat, which provides detailed insights into your competitors' online advertising strategies. With Adbeat, you track your competitors' ad placements across various networks, analyze their ad copy and creative, and even see which keywords they are targeting. This piece of information helps you identify new opportunities for your own campaigns and stay one step ahead of the competition.

Another important metric to consider when analyzing your online advertising campaigns is click-through rate (CTR). CTR measures the percentage of people who click on your ad after seeing it, and is a key indicator of how engaging your ad is to your target audience. By monitoring your CTR and comparing it to industry benchmarks, you identify areas for improvement in your ad creative and targeting strategies.

In addition to CTR, other important metrics to consider when analyzing your online advertising campaigns include conversion rate, cost per acquisition (CPA), and return on ad spend (ROAS). By tracking these metrics and using competitive ad intelligence tools to gain insights into your competitors' strategies, you optimize your online advertising campaigns for maximum effectiveness and stay ahead of the competition.

Overall, competitive ad intelligence tools and metrics are essential for gaining a competitive edge in the crowded online advertising space. By using these tools to track your competitors' strategies and analyze key metrics like CTR, conversion rate, and ROAS, you ensure that your online advertising campaigns are performing at their best and driving maximum results for your business.

F. Case Studies - Examining real-world examples to illustrate successes and failures in traditional Digital ad analytics.

In the world of advertising, understanding the success and failures of traditional ad analytics is crucial for businesses looking to optimize their marketing strategies. Case studies provide valuable insights into real-world examples, showcasing how different companies have utilized competitive ad intelligence to their advantage.

Success Story: Company A, a leading retail brand, used traditional digital analytics to track the ad placements and copy decision of their top competitors. By analyzing the data, Company A was able to identify gaps in the market and develop targeted campaigns that resonated with their target audience. As a result, they saw a significant increase in brand awareness and sales, surpassing their competitors in the marketplace.

Failure Story: Company B, a tech startup, neglected to invest in traditional ad analytics and relied solely on its own analytics to guide its marketing efforts. Without a clear understanding of what its competitors were doing, Company B struggled to differentiate its brand and target audience. As a result, it saw minimal growth and struggled to compete in a crowded market.

By examining these case studies, businesses saw the tangible impact traditional ad analytics had on their marketing strategies. Whether it's identifying new opportunities for growth or avoiding costly mistakes, leveraging real-world examples help businesses make informed decisions and stay ahead of the competition.

Section: 3. Market Dynamics: Understanding the Competitive Landscape through Ad Intelligence

In the fast-paced world of digital advertising, staying ahead of the competition is crucial. One way to gain a competitive edge is through the use of competitive ad intelligence. By analyzing the advertising strategies of your competitors, you gain valuable insights into market dynamics and make informed decisions to drive your own success.

Competitive ad intelligence allows you to monitor the advertising activities of your competitors, including the types of ads they are running, the platforms they are using, and the messaging they are employing. By analyzing the data, you identify trends in the market, understand your competitors' positioning, and uncover new opportunities for growth.

One key aspect of market dynamics is that competitive ad intelligence helps you understand pricing strategies. By monitoring the pricing of your competitors' products or services, you gain insights into how they are positioning themselves in the market and adjust your own pricing strategy accordingly.

Another important aspect of market dynamics is consumer behavior. By analyzing the ad creative and messaging of your competitors, you gain insights into what resonates with consumers and tailor your own messaging to better meet their needs and preferences.

Overall, competitive ad intelligence is a powerful tool for understanding market dynamics and gaining a competitive edge in the digital landscape. By leveraging the data, you make informed decisions that drive success and growth for your business.

A. Industry Trends and Innovations

In today's fast-paced and ever-evolving business landscape, staying ahead of industry trends and innovations is crucial for companies looking to maintain a competitive edge. One key tool that helps businesses stay on top of the latest developments in their industry is competitive ad intelligence.

Competitive ad intelligence involves monitoring and analyzing the advertising strategies and campaigns of competitors in order to gain insights into their marketing tactics and performance. By keeping a close eye on what competitors are doing in terms of brand advertising, companies identify emerging trends, spot potential opportunities, and make more informed decisions about their own marketing strategies.

One of the most significant industry trends that has emerged in recent years is the shift towards digital advertising. As consumers spend more time online, companies are increasingly investing in digital channels such as social media, search engine marketing, and display advertising to reach their target audiences. By leveraging competitive ad intelligence tools, businesses track how competitors are leveraging digital advertising and identify opportunities to improve their own online presence.

Another key innovation in the advertising industry is the rise of programmatic advertising. This automated, data-driven approach to buying and placing ads has revolutionized the way companies target and reach consumers. By using competitive ad intelligence to monitor how competitors are utilizing programmatic advertising, businesses stay on top of this rapidly evolving trend and ensure they are not falling behind in their digital advertising efforts.

Summary

Staying abreast of industry trends and innovations is essential for businesses looking to succeed in today's competitive marketplace. By utilizing competitive ad intelligence tools to monitor competitors' advertising strategies, companies gain valuable insights that inform their own marketing decisions and help them stay ahead of the curve.

B. Impact on Advertising Strategies - Investigating how market dynamics influence the formulation of effective advertising strategies.

In today's competitive business landscape, advertising plays a crucial role in helping companies stand out and attract customers. With the rise of digital advertising and the increasing complexity of consumer behavior, understanding the impact of market dynamics on advertising strategies is more important than ever.

One key aspect of developing successful advertising strategies is competitive ad intelligence. By analyzing the advertising tactics of competitors, companies gain valuable insights into what works and what doesn't in their industry. This piece of information helps them identify gaps in the market, understand consumer preferences, and fine-tune their own advertising efforts to better reach their target audience.

Market dynamics, such as changes in consumer behavior, emerging trends, and competitive pressures, significantly influence the effectiveness of advertising strategies. For example, a sudden shift in consumer preferences towards eco-friendly products may prompt companies to adjust their messaging and focus on sustainability in their advertising campaigns.

Furthermore, understanding the competitive landscape is essential for companies to stay ahead of the curve and differentiate themselves from rivals. By monitoring the advertising strategies of competitors, companies identify opportunities to capitalize on market trends, target new customer segments, and optimize their advertising spend for maximum impact.

Summary

The impact of market dynamics on advertising strategies is undeniable. By leveraging competitive ad intelligence and staying attuned to changes in the market, companies develop more effective advertising campaigns that resonate with their target audience and drive business growth.

Section: 4. Consumer Behavior Analysis

Consumer behavior analysis is a crucial aspect of any advertising strategy. By understanding how consumers think, feel, and act, businesses tailor their products and services to meet the needs and desires of their target audience. One way to gain insight into consumer behavior is through competitive ad intelligence.

Competitive ad intelligence involves monitoring and analyzing the advertising strategies of competitors in order to gain a competitive edge. By studying the ads that competitors are running, businesses learn valuable information about consumer preferences, trends, and buying habits. This piece of information is used to create more effective and targeted advertising campaigns.

One key benefit of competitive ad intelligence is that it allows businesses to stay ahead of the competition. By keeping a close eye on what competitors are doing, companies identify gaps in the market and capitalize on new opportunities. Additionally, by understanding the messaging and imagery that resonates with consumers, businesses create more compelling ads that drive engagement and conversions.

Summary

Consumer behavior analysis is essential for businesses looking to succeed in today's competitive market. By utilizing competitive ad intelligence, companies gain valuable insights into consumer behavior and create more effective advertising campaigns that drive results. By staying informed and adapting to changing consumer preferences, businesses stay ahead of the competition and thrive in the ever-evolving marketplace.

A. The Psychology of Consumer Decision-making

Consumer decision-making is a complex process that is influenced by a variety of psychological factors. In today's competitive market, understanding these factors is crucial for businesses looking to gain a competitive edge. One key aspect of this understanding is through competitive ad intelligence, which involves analyzing the advertising strategies of competitors to gain insights into consumer behavior.

One important psychological factor that influences consumer decision-making is the concept of social proof. This is the idea that people are more likely to make a purchase if they see others doing the same. By analyzing the social media advertising strategies of competitors, businesses gain valuable insights into how they are using social proof to influence consumers.

Another important psychological factor is the concept of scarcity. Consumers are more likely to make a purchase if they believe that the product is in limited supply. By studying the social media advertising strategies of competitors, businesses examine how the concept of scarcity is used as a marketing tactic to inform their own advertising strategies.

Additionally, understanding the role of emotions in consumer decision-making is crucial for businesses looking to effectively market their products. By analyzing the social media advertising strategies of competitors, businesses gain insights into how they are appealing to consumers' emotions and use this piece of information to create more impactful advertising campaigns.

Summary

Understanding the psychology of consumer decision-making is essential for businesses looking to succeed in today's competitive market. By utilizing competitive ad intelligence and analyzing the social media advertising strategies of competitors, businesses gain valuable insights into consumer behavior and tailor their marketing strategies accordingly.

B. Utilizing Behavioral Data in Competitive Ad Intelligence

In the world of digital advertising, understanding consumer behavior is crucial for staying ahead of the competition. By analyzing behavioral data, marketers gain valuable insights into their target audience's preferences, interests, and purchasing habits. This piece of information is used to create more targeted and effective advertising campaigns.

One powerful tool for utilizing behavioral data in competitive ad intelligence is competitive ad intelligence software such as Similarweb, Nielsen Ad Intel, Media Radar to mention a few. The software allows marketers to track and analyze their competitors' advertising strategies, including the keywords they are targeting, the ad placements they are using, and the messaging they are using to attract customers.

By leveraging competitive ad intelligence software, marketers gain a deeper understanding of their competitors' tactics and identify opportunities to outperform them. For example, by analyzing the keywords that competitors are targeting, marketers identify gaps in the market that they can exploit to reach new audiences.

Furthermore, by monitoring their competitors' ad placements and messaging, marketers identify trends and best practices they can incorporate into their own campaigns. This helps them optimize their advertising efforts and maximize their return on investment.

Summary

Utilizing behavioral data in competitive ad intelligence is essential for staying competitive in today's crowded digital marketplace. By leveraging tools like competitive ad intelligence software, marketers gain valuable insights into their competitors' strategies and identify opportunities to outperform them. By analyzing behavioral data and incorporating them into their advertising campaigns, marketers create more targeted and effective campaigns that resonate with their target audience.

C. Personalization and Targeting Strategies

In today's digital advertising landscape, personalization and targeting strategies are crucial for reaching and engaging with the right audience. With the help of competitive ad intelligence, businesses gain valuable insights into their competitors' advertising tactics and use this piece of information to enhance their own marketing efforts.

One of the key benefits of using competitive ad intelligence for personalization and targeting is the ability to understand what messages resonate with your target audience. By analyzing your competitors' ads, you identify common themes, messaging strategies, and calls to action that are effective in driving engagement and conversions.

Furthermore, competitive ad intelligence allows you to track your competitors' targeting strategies, including the demographics, interests, and behaviors of their audience. This piece of information helps you refine your own targeting efforts to ensure that you are reaching the right people with the right message at the right time.

Another advantage of leveraging competitive ad intelligence for personalization and targeting is the ability to stay ahead of industry trends and innovations. By monitoring your competitors' advertising campaigns, you identify emerging trends, new technologies, and creative strategies that are driving success in your industry.

Summary

Overall, personalization and targeting strategies are essential for maximizing the impact of your advertising campaigns. By using competitive ad intelligence to gain insights into your competitors' tactics, you optimize your own marketing efforts, reach the right audience, and stay ahead of the competition.

Section: 5. Data-Driven Decision Making: How Competitive Ad Intelligence Transforms Strategy

In today's fast-paced digital landscape, businesses are constantly seeking ways to gain a competitive edge. One powerful tool that helps companies make informed decisions is competitive ad intelligence. By utilizing data-driven insights from competitors' advertising strategies, businesses better understand market trends, consumer behavior, and industry benchmarks.

Competitive ad intelligence allows businesses to track and analyze their competitors' advertising campaigns across various channels, such as social media, search engines, and display ads. By monitoring key metrics like ad spend, engagement rates, and audience demographics, businesses gain valuable insights into what strategies are working for their competitors and how they can improve their own campaigns.

One of the key benefits of using competitive ad intelligence for data-driven decision making is the ability to identify new opportunities for growth. By analyzing competitors' ad strategies, businesses uncover untapped markets, new trends, and emerging consumer preferences. This piece of information helps companies tailor their own advertising efforts to better meet the needs and interests of their target audience.

Furthermore, competitive ad intelligence also helps businesses optimize their advertising budgets by identifying which channels and tactics are delivering the best results. By analyzing competitors' ad spend and performance metrics, companies allocate their resources more effectively and maximize their ROI.

Summary

Overall, competitive ad intelligence is a valuable tool for businesses looking to make data-driven decisions and stay ahead of the competition. By leveraging insights from competitors' advertising strategies, companies gain a deeper understanding of their market, identify new growth opportunities, and optimize their advertising efforts for maximum impact.

A. Leveraging Big Data for Ad Insights

In today's digital age, businesses are constantly striving to stay ahead of the competition. One way to gain a competitive edge is by leveraging big data for ad insights. By utilizing competitive ad intelligence, companies gain valuable information about their competitors' advertising strategies and use the data to inform their own marketing efforts.

Competitive ad intelligence involves analyzing the ads and campaigns of competitors to identify trends, strengths, and weaknesses. This piece of information helps businesses understand what is working in the market, what their competitors are doing right, and where there are opportunities for improvement.

By tapping into big data sources such as social media, online advertising platforms, digital advertising intelligence software and market research reports, companies gather a wealth of information about their competitors' ad strategies. The data are used to track competitor ad spending, monitor ad performance, and identify key messaging and targeting tactics.

With this piece of information in hand, businesses make more informed decisions about their own advertising efforts. They tailor their messaging and targeting to better reach their target audience, optimize their ad spend to maximize ROI, and stay ahead of the competition in an increasingly crowded marketplace.

Summary

Leveraging big data for ad insights through competitive ad intelligence provide businesses with a valuable competitive advantage. By analyzing the ads and campaigns of competitors, businesses gain valuable insights that inform their own marketing strategies and help them stand out in a crowded market.

B. Implementing Advanced Analytics Tools for Competitive Ad Intelligence

In today's highly competitive business landscape, having access to advanced analytics tools is essential for staying ahead of the competition. One key area where these tools make a significant impact is in competitive ad intelligence. By utilizing advanced analytics tools, businesses gain valuable insights into their competitors' advertising strategies and make more informed decisions about their own marketing efforts.

Here are some key areas to consider when implementing advanced analytics tools for competitive ad intelligence:

1. Understanding the Competitive Landscape: Before diving into competitive ad intelligence, it's important to have a clear understanding of the competitive landscape. This involves identifying key competitors, analyzing their advertising strategies, and determining their strengths and weaknesses.

2. Choosing the Right Analytics Tools: There are a wide range of advanced analytics tools available for competitive ad intelligence, each offering different features and capabilities. It's important to choose the right tools that align with your business goals.

3. Gathering Data: Once you have selected the right analytics tools, the next step is to start gathering data on your competitors' advertising activities. This includes tracking ad placements, ad copy, ad spend, and audience demographics.

4. Analyzing Data: After collecting data on your competitors' advertising efforts, the next step is to analyze the data to gain valuable insights. This involves identifying trends, patterns, and opportunities for improvement in your own advertising strategies.

5. Implementing Changes: Based on the insights gained from competitive ad intelligence, it's important to implement changes to your own advertising strategies. This involves adjusting ad placements, refining ad copy, or reallocating ad spend to better reach your target audience.

By implementing advanced analytics tools for competitive ad intelligence, businesses gain a competitive edge in the marketplace and make more informed decisions about their advertising strategies. With access to valuable insights into their competitors' advertising efforts, businesses better position themselves for success and drive better results from their advertising campaigns.

C. Real-time Decision-Making in Advertising

Competitive ad intelligence is a crucial tool for real-time decision-making in advertising. In today's fast-paced digital world, brands are constantly vying for consumer attention, making it essential to monitor and analyze competitors' advertising strategies in real-time.

One key benefit of competitive ad intelligence is the ability to stay ahead of the competition by identifying trends and opportunities as they happen. By tracking competitors' ad placements, messaging, and creative content, brands quickly adjust their own advertising campaigns to stay relevant and competitive.

Another advantage of competitive ad intelligence is the ability to optimize advertising spend by identifying which channels and platforms are most effective for reaching target audiences. By analyzing competitors' ad performance metrics, brands make data-driven decisions on where to allocate their advertising budget for maximum impact.

Furthermore, competitive ad intelligence allows brands to benchmark their own performance against competitors and industry standards. By comparing key metrics such as ad engagement rates, click-through rates, and conversion rates, brands identify areas for improvement and refine their advertising strategies for better results.

Summary

Overall, competitive ad intelligence is a powerful tool for real-time decision-making in advertising. By monitoring competitors' strategies, optimizing advertising spend, and benchmarking performance, brands stay ahead of the competition and drive success in today's competitive advertising landscape.

Section: 6. Competitive Ad Intelligence: A New Paradigm

In today's digital age, the landscape of advertising is constantly evolving. With the rise of online business platforms and the increasing competition among brands, it has become more crucial than ever for businesses to stay ahead of the curve when it comes to their advertising strategies. This is where competitive ad intelligence comes into play.

Competitive ad intelligence refers to the practice of monitoring and analyzing the advertising activities of competitors in order to gain insights and stay competitive in the market. By keeping a close eye on what your competitors are doing in terms of advertising, you can identify trends, understand their strategies, and ultimately make more informed decisions for your own campaigns.

One of the key advantages of competitive ad intelligence is that it allows businesses to benchmark their performance against their competitors. By comparing metrics such as ad spend, ad placement, and ad creative, you gain a better understanding of where you stand in relation to your competitors and identify areas for improvement.

Furthermore, competitive ad intelligence also helps businesses identify new opportunities for growth and innovation. By analyzing the strategies and tactics that are working for your competitors, you adapt and optimize your own campaigns to stay ahead of the curve.

Summary

Competitive ad intelligence represents a new paradigm in advertising. By leveraging the power of data and insights, businesses gain a competitive edge in the market and drive better results for their advertising campaigns. So, if you want to stay ahead of the competition, it's time to embrace the power of competitive ad intelligence.

A. Defining Competitive Ad Intelligence

Competitive ad intelligence is a crucial component of any successful advertising strategy. By closely monitoring and analyzing the campaigns of your competitors, you gain valuable insights into their tactics and identify opportunities to outperform them in the marketplace.

One key aspect of competitive ad intelligence is understanding the messaging and creative elements that your competitors are using in their ads. By studying their copywriting, imagery, and calls to action, you identify trends and patterns that influence consumer behavior. This piece of information help you refine your own ad campaigns and stay ahead of the competition.

Another important aspect of competitive ad intelligence is monitoring where and how your competitors are advertising. By tracking the platforms and channels they are using, you identify new opportunities for reaching your target audience. Additionally, analyzing the frequency and timing of their ads help you optimize your own advertising schedule for maximum impact.

In addition, competitive ad intelligence provides valuable insights into your competitors' targeting strategies. By analyzing the demographics, interests, and behaviors of the audiences they are reaching, you better understand who your competitors are trying to reach and tailor your own targeting efforts accordingly.

Summary

Overall, competitive ad intelligence is a powerful tool for staying ahead of the competition and maximizing the effectiveness of your advertising efforts. By closely monitoring your competitors' ads and strategies, you identify opportunities for improvement and develop a more competitive and compelling advertising strategy.

1. Understanding Competitors Beyond Analytics

When it comes to understanding competitors, many businesses rely solely on analytics to gather information. While analytics provides valuable insights into a competitor's performance, it is important to look beyond just the numbers to truly understand what makes a competitor successful. This is where competitive ad intelligence comes into play.

Competitive ad intelligence involves analyzing a competitor's advertising strategies, messaging, and overall brand presence to gain a deeper understanding of their advertising tactics. By studying the ads that a competitor is running across various platforms, businesses uncover valuable insights into their target audience, messaging, and overall brand positioning.

One key aspect of competitive ad intelligence is understanding the competitive landscape. By analyzing the ads of multiple competitors within an industry, businesses identify trends, gaps in the market, and potential opportunities for differentiation. This helps businesses fine-tune their own advertising strategies and stay ahead of the competition.

Another important aspect of competitive ad intelligence is understanding the messaging and positioning of competitors. By analyzing the language, imagery, and overall tone of a competitor's ads, businesses gain insights into their brand values, target audience, and overall advertising strategy. This helps businesses better position themselves in the market and create more effective advertising campaigns.

Summary

Overall, competitive ad intelligence is a valuable tool for businesses looking to gain a deeper understanding of their competitors and the overall competitive landscape. By going beyond analytics, businesses uncover valuable insights that help them stay ahead of the competition and drive success in their industry.

2. Incorporating Competitive Intelligence into Advertising Strategy

Competitive intelligence plays a crucial role in shaping a successful advertising strategy. By analyzing the advertising tactics of your competitors, you gain valuable insights into what is working well in the market and what strategies are falling flat. In this segment, I will explore the importance of incorporating competitive intelligence into your advertising strategy and how you use competitive ad intelligence to stay ahead of the game.

Understanding your competitors' advertising strategies you identify gaps in the market that you capitalize on. By monitoring their ad placements, messaging, and targeting, you uncover opportunities to differentiate your brand and stand out from the competition. Additionally, analyzing the performance of your competitors' ads provides valuable insights into what resonates with your target audience and help you fine-tune your own messaging for better results.

One of the key benefits of competitive ad intelligence is the ability to track trends and stay up-to-date with the latest industry developments. By keeping a close eye on your competitors' advertising activities, you identify emerging trends and adjust your strategy accordingly. This helps you stay ahead of the curve and maintain a competitive edge in the market.

Incorporating competitive intelligence into your advertising strategy helps you optimize your ad spend and maximize ROI. By analyzing your competitors' ad placements and performance metrics, you identify high-performing channels and target audiences that are worth investing in. This helps you allocate your budget more effectively and ensure that your advertising efforts are generating the desired results.

Summary

Overall, competitive ad intelligence is a powerful tool that helps you stay ahead of the competition and drive success in your advertising campaigns. By analyzing your competitors' strategies, tracking industry trends, and optimizing your ad spend, you create a more effective and impactful advertising strategy that delivers results. So, don't underestimate the power of competitive intelligence in shaping your advertising strategy – it could be the key to unlocking your brand's full potential.

B. Components of Competitive Ad Intelligence

When it comes to staying ahead in the world of digital advertising, having a strong understanding of your competitors' strategies is key. This is where competitive ad intelligence comes into play. By analyzing your competitors' ads and campaigns, you gain valuable insights that help you improve your own advertising efforts.

There are several key components of competitive ad intelligence that you should be aware of. These include:

1. Ad Creatives: One of the most important aspects of competitive ad intelligence is analyzing your competitors' ad creatives. By studying the design, messaging, and calls to action of their ads, you get a better understanding of what resonates with your target audience and how to improve your own ad creatives.

2. Ad Placement: Another important component of competitive ad intelligence is analyzing where your competitors are placing their ads. By understanding which platforms and channels they are using, you identify new opportunities for reaching your target audience and expanding your advertising reach.

3. Ad Spend: Monitoring your competitors' ad spend provides valuable insights into their advertising strategies. By tracking how much they are spending on ads and where they are allocating their budget, you make more informed decisions about your own ad spend and budget allocation.

4. Ad Performance: Finally, competitive ad intelligence involves analyzing the performance of your competitors' ads. By tracking metrics such as click-through rates, conversion rates, and ROI, you gain a better understanding of what is working (and what isn't) in your industry and use this piece of information to optimize your own ad campaigns.

Summary

Competitive ad intelligence is a crucial component of any successful digital advertising strategy. By analyzing your competitors' ad creatives, placement, spend, and performance, you gain valuable insights that help you improve your own advertising efforts and stay ahead of the competition.

1. Ad Creatives Analysis

In the world of digital advertising, understanding your competitors' ad creatives is crucial for staying ahead of the game. By conducting a thorough analysis of your competitors' ad creatives, you gain valuable insights into what strategies are working for them and how you can improve your own campaigns.

Competitive ad intelligence tools provide you with detailed information about your competitors' ads. These tools show you the ad copy, images, and calls-to-action that your competitors are using, as well as information about where and when their ads are running.

By using competitive ad intelligence tools, you identify trends in your industry and see what types of ad creatives are resonating with your target audience. You also track your competitors' ad performance over time and see how their strategies are evolving.

Armed with this piece of information, you make more informed decisions about your own ad creatives and optimize your campaigns for maximum impact. By staying on top of your competitors' ad creatives and constantly analyzing and refining your own strategies, you ensure that your advertising efforts are always one step ahead of the competition.

Summary

Conducting a thorough analysis of your competitors' ad creatives using competitive ad intelligence tools is essential for success in the world of digital advertising. By staying informed about your competitors' strategies and constantly refining your own, you ensure that your campaigns are always fresh, engaging, and effective.

2. Uncovering Successful Creative Strategies

In today's fast-paced and competitive business landscape, staying ahead of the game is crucial for success. One powerful tool that helps businesses uncover successful creative strategies is competitive ad intelligence.

Competitive ad intelligence involves analyzing and monitoring the advertising strategies of competitors in order to gain insights and inspiration for your own campaigns. By keeping a close eye on what your competitors are doing, you identify trends, see what is working (and what isn't), and ultimately develop more effective advertising strategies.

One key benefit of competitive ad intelligence is that it allows you to stay informed about the latest industry trends and innovations. By studying the advertising tactics of your competitors, you gain valuable insights into what is resonating with consumers and adapt your own strategies accordingly.

Additionally, competitive ad intelligence helps you identify gaps in the market that your competitors may be overlooking. By analyzing their ad campaigns, you uncover opportunities to differentiate your brand and stand out from the competition.

Furthermore, competitive ad intelligence provides valuable benchmarking data to help you track your own performance and measure the success of your advertising efforts. By comparing your campaigns to those of your competitors, you identify areas for improvement and optimize your strategies for better results.

Summary

Competitive ad intelligence is a powerful tool for uncovering successful creative strategies in today's competitive marketplace. By leveraging this valuable insight, businesses stay ahead of the curve, identify opportunities for growth, and ultimately achieve greater success in their advertising efforts.

3. Analyzing Design Elements, Messaging, and Calls-to-action in Competitive Ad Intelligence

When it comes to creating successful ad campaigns, understanding and analyzing design elements, messaging, and calls-to-action is crucial. By using competitive ad intelligence, marketers gain valuable insights into what works and what doesn't in the world of advertising.

Design Elements:

One of the first things that consumers notice about an ad is its design. From colors and fonts to images and layout, the design elements of an ad play a significant role in capturing the attention of the audience. By analyzing the design elements of competitors' ads, marketers identify trends, best practices, and opportunities to stand out from the crowd.

Messaging:

The messaging of an ad is what conveys the brand's value proposition and resonates with the target audience. By analyzing the messaging of competitors' ads, marketers gain insights into what language, tone, and messaging strategies are most effective in their industry. This piece of information helps marketers craft compelling and persuasive messaging that drives action.

Calls-to-action:

The call-to-action (CTA) is arguably the most important element of an ad, as it tells the audience what action to take next. By analyzing the CTAs of competitors' ads, marketers learn what types of CTAs are most effective in driving conversions. Whether it's a simple "Shop Now" button or a more creative CTA, understanding what works in the competitive landscape helps marketers optimize their own CTAs for maximum impact.

Summary

Analyzing design elements, messaging, and calls-to-action using competitive ad intelligence provides marketers with valuable insights that inform their own ad campaigns. By staying informed about what's working in the industry, marketers create more effective and successful ads that resonate with their target audience.

2. Target Audience Insights

When it comes to creating successful advertising campaigns, understanding your target audience is key. By utilizing competitive ad intelligence, you gain valuable insights into the preferences and behaviors of your target audience. This piece of information helps you tailor your messaging and marketing strategies to better resonate with potential customers.

One important aspect of competitive ad intelligence is analyzing the ads and messaging used by your competitors. By studying the ads that are resonating with your target audience, you gain a better understanding of what types of messaging and visuals that are most effective. This helps you craft your own ads that are more likely to capture the attention of your target audience.

Additionally, competitive ad intelligence provides insights into the demographics and psychographics of your target audience. By analyzing the ads that are targeted towards specific segments of the population, you have a better understanding of your target audience and what they are looking for in a product or service. This piece of information helps you create more targeted and personalized advertising campaigns that are more likely to resonate with your audience.

Summary

Overall, competitive ad intelligence is a valuable tool for gaining insights into your target audience and creating more effective advertising campaigns. By analyzing the ads and messaging used by your competitors, you have a better understanding of what resonates with your audience and tailor your own campaigns to meet their needs and preferences.

A. Identifying Competitor Target Demographics

Need to identify competitor target demographics, competitive ad intelligence is a powerful tool that provide valuable insights. By analyzing the advertising strategies of your competitors, you gain a better understanding of their target audience and tailor your own marketing efforts accordingly.

One key aspect of competitive ad intelligence is analyzing the types of ads that your competitors are running. By examining the content, messaging, and visuals of these ads, you can start to paint a picture of who they are trying to reach. Are they targeting a specific age group, gender, or geographic location? Are they appealing to a particular lifestyle or interest? By answering these questions, you begin to identify the demographic characteristics of your competitors' target audience.

Another important aspect of competitive ad intelligence is tracking where your competitors are advertising. Are they running ads on social media platforms, search engines, or websites? By monitoring their advertising placements, you gain insights into the channels that are most effective for reaching their target audience. This piece of information helps you optimize your own advertising strategy and focus on the channels that are most likely to reach your target demographic.

In addition to analyzing the content and placement of your competitors' ads, competitive ad intelligence also helps you track the performance of their campaigns. By monitoring key metrics such as click-through rates, conversion rates, and engagement levels, you gain a better understanding of how effective their advertising efforts are at reaching their target audience. This piece of information helps you benchmark your own performance against your competitors and identify areas for improvement.

Summary

Overall, competitive ad intelligence is a valuable tool for identifying competitor target demographics. By analyzing the advertising strategies of your competitors, you gain valuable insights into who they are trying to reach, where they are advertising, and how effective their campaigns are. Armed with this piece of information, you tailor your own advertising efforts to better target your desired demographic and gain a competitive edge in the marketplace.

B. Leveraging Keywords for Better Targeting

In today's digital age, leveraging audience data for better targeting is crucial for businesses looking to reach their target audience effectively. One powerful tool that helps businesses achieve this is competitive ad intelligence.

Competitive ad intelligence allows businesses to gather insights on their competitors' advertising strategies, including the keywords they are targeting, the ad copy they are using, and the platforms they are advertising on. By analyzing the data, businesses gain a better understanding of their industry landscape and identify opportunities to improve their own targeting efforts.

One key benefit of leveraging competitive ad intelligence for better targeting is the ability to identify new keywords opportunities. By analyzing the keywords that competitors are targeting, businesses uncover keywords that they may not have thought of themselves. This helps businesses expand their reach and attract new customers who are searching for products or services related to these keywords.

Additionally, competitive ad intelligence helps businesses optimize their ad copy for better targeting. By analyzing the ad copy that competitors are using, businesses gain insights into the messaging that resonates with their target audience. This helps businesses craft more compelling ad copy that effectively communicates their value proposition and drives conversions.

Furthermore, competitive ad intelligence helps businesses identify the most effective advertising platforms for reaching their keywords target audience. By analyzing where competitors are advertising, businesses determine which platforms are most popular among their keywords target audience and allocate their advertising budget accordingly.

Summary

Leveraging competitive ad intelligence for better keywords targeting helps businesses improve their advertising strategies and reach their target audience more effectively. By analyzing competitors' advertising strategies, businesses uncover new keywords opportunities, optimize their ad copy, and identify the most effective advertising platforms. Ultimately, this leads to increased brand awareness, higher conversion rates, and greater success in the digital marketplace.

3. Ad Placement and Channel Strategy

In creating strategic advertising, one of the most important aspects to consider is where and how you place your ads. This is where competitive ad intelligence is a game-changer. By analyzing your competitors' ad placements and strategies, you gain valuable insights into what works and what doesn't in your industry.

One key aspect of ad placement is choosing the right channels to reach your target audience. This involves understanding where your audience spends their time and tailoring your ad placements accordingly. For example, if your target audience is active on social media, you may want to focus on placing ads on platforms like Facebook or Instagram. On the other hand, if your audience is more likely to engage with traditional media, you may want to consider placing ads on TV or radio, or on interconnected TV if the programmatic advertising option is chosen.

Another important consideration is the timing of your ad placements. By analyzing your competitors' ad strategies, you identify the times when they are most active and adjust your own ad placements accordingly. This helps you maximize the impact of your ads and reach your audience at the most opportune moments.

In addition to channel selection and timing, competitive ad intelligence also helps you optimize your ad creatives. By analyzing your competitors' ad designs and messaging, you gain inspiration for your own ads and ensure that they stand out from the competition.

Summary

Ad placement and channel strategy are crucial components of a successful advertising campaign. By leveraging competitive ad intelligence, you gain valuable insights into your competitors' strategies and optimize your own ad placements for maximum impact.

A. Analyzing Where Competitors Are Advertising

If you want to stay ahead in the competitive business landscape, it's crucial to keep a close eye on where your competitors are advertising. By utilizing competitive ad intelligence tools, you gain valuable insights into the strategies that your rivals are using to reach their target audience.

One key aspect of analyzing where your competitors are advertising is understanding the platforms they are utilizing. Are they focusing on traditional channels such as television and print ads, or are they investing heavily in digital advertising efforts such as social media and paid search advertising? By identifying where your competitors are allocating their advertising budget, you make informed decisions about where to focus your own efforts.

Another important factor to consider when analyzing your competitors' advertising strategies is the messaging they are using. Are they highlighting specific features or benefits of their products or services? Are they leveraging emotional appeals or focusing on price promotions? By studying the content of your competitors' ads, you gain valuable insights into the messaging that resonates with your target audience and tailor your own advertising accordingly.

Additionally, it's important to pay attention to the frequency and timing of your competitors' ads. Are they running continuous campaigns, burst pattern or seasonal promotions? Are they targeting specific times of day or days of the week to reach their audience? By monitoring the media strategy of your competitors' advertising efforts, you identify opportunities to stand out and capture the attention of your target audience.

Summary

Analyzing where your competitors are advertising using competitive ad intelligence tools provides valuable insights into their strategies and helps you make informed decisions about your own advertising efforts. By staying vigilant and proactive in monitoring your rivals' activities, you position your business for success in the competitive marketplace.

B. Optimizing Ad Placement for Maximum Impact

In maximizing the impact of your ad placements, one key strategy to consider is utilizing competitive ad intelligence. By analyzing the ads of your competitors and understanding their placement strategies, you gain valuable insights to inform your own ad placement decisions.

One important aspect to consider when optimizing ad placement is understanding where your target audience spends their time online. By using competitive ad intelligence tools, you identify the websites and platforms that your competitors are advertising on, and use this piece of information to strategically place your own ads in those same locations.

Another key factor to consider is the timing of your ad placements. By monitoring when your competitors are running their ads, you identify peak times for reaching your target audience and ensure that your ads are seen at the most effective times.

Additionally, analyzing the design and messaging of your competitors' ads provides valuable inspiration for optimizing your own ad creatives. By understanding what resonates with your target audience, you tailor your ad placements to maximize impact and drive better results.

Summary

Utilizing competitive ad intelligence provides valuable insights to inform your ad placement strategy and maximize the impact of your advertising efforts. By analyzing the ads of your competitors, understanding where and when they are placing their ads, and taking inspiration from their creative approaches, you optimize your ad placements for maximum impact and drive better results for your campaigns.

Section: 7. Tools and Technologies for Competitive Ad Intelligence

In staying ahead of the competition in the world of advertising, having access to the right tools and technologies for competitive ad intelligence is essential. By utilizing these resources, businesses gain valuable insights into their competitors' strategies and make more informed decisions about their own advertising campaigns.

One of the most important tools for competitive ad intelligence is a competitive analysis platform. These platforms allow businesses to track their competitors' ad campaigns across various channels, such as social media, search engines, and display advertising. By analyzing the messaging, creative elements, and targeting strategies used by competitors, businesses identify opportunities to differentiate themselves and improve their own campaigns.

Another essential tool for competitive ad intelligence is ad tracking software. This software allows businesses to monitor their competitors' ad placements, ad formats, and performance metrics in real-time. By keeping a close eye on what their competitors are doing, businesses adjust their own campaigns accordingly and stay one step ahead in the advertising game.

In addition to these tools, businesses also leverage technologies such as artificial intelligence and machine learning to enhance their competitive ad intelligence efforts. These technologies analyze vast amounts of data to identify patterns, trends, and opportunities that may not be immediately apparent to human analysts. By harnessing the power of AI and machine learning, businesses gain a deeper understanding of their competitors' strategies and make smarter decisions about their own advertising efforts.

Summary

Having access to the right tools and technologies for competitive ad intelligence is crucial for businesses looking to succeed in today's competitive advertising landscape. By leveraging competitive analysis platforms, ad tracking software, and cutting-edge technologies like AI and machine learning, businesses gain valuable insights into their competitors' strategies and make more informed decisions about their own advertising campaigns. With the right tools and technologies at their disposal, businesses stay ahead of the competition and achieve success in their advertising efforts.

A. Advanced Analytics Platforms

In today's digital age, businesses are constantly looking for ways to gain a competitive edge in the market. One of the most effective ways to do this is through advanced analytics platforms that provide insights into competitors' advertising strategies. By utilizing competitive ad intelligence, businesses better understand their competitors' tactics and make more informed decisions about their own advertising campaigns.

Competitive ad intelligence is the process of gathering and analyzing data on competitors' advertising strategies. This includes information on the types of ads they are running, where they are being displayed, and how they are performing. By using advanced analytics platforms, businesses gain valuable insights into their competitors' tactics and use this information to improve their own advertising campaigns.

Advanced analytics platforms offer a wide range of tools and features that help businesses gather and analyze competitive ad intelligence. These platforms use data from various sources, such as social media, search engines, and ad networks, to provide a comprehensive view of competitors' advertising strategies. By using these platforms, businesses track their competitors' ads in real-time, monitor their performance, and identify trends and patterns in their advertising tactics.

In addition to providing insights into competitors' advertising strategies, advanced analytics platforms also help businesses optimize their own advertising campaigns. By analyzing data on ad performance, audience engagement, and competitor tactics, businesses make data-driven decisions about their own advertising strategies. This leads to improved ROI, increased brand visibility, and a stronger competitive edge in the market.

Summary

Advanced analytics platforms play a crucial role in helping businesses gain a competitive edge through competitive ad intelligence. By utilizing these platforms, businesses better understand their competitors' advertising strategies, optimize their own campaigns, and make more informed decisions about their marketing efforts. With the right tools and insights, businesses stay ahead of the competition and achieve their advertising goals.

B. Overview of Cutting-edge Analytics Tools

In the competitive ad intelligence landscape, staying ahead of the curve is crucial for businesses looking to gain a competitive edge. This is where cutting-edge analytics tools come into play, offering advanced capabilities to analyze and optimize advertising strategies.

One of the key tools in this space is competitive ad intelligence software, which provides valuable insights into the advertising strategies of competitors. These tools allow businesses to monitor the ad campaigns of their rivals, track their performance metrics, and identify areas for improvement in their own advertising efforts.

Another important aspect of cutting-edge analytics tools is their ability to provide real-time data and actionable insights. By leveraging advanced analytics techniques such as machine learning and predictive modeling, businesses make data-driven decisions that drive better results.

Furthermore, these tools often come with customizable dashboards and reporting capabilities, allowing users to visualize and analyze data in a way that is tailored to their specific needs. This not only makes it easier to understand complex data sets but also enables businesses to quickly identify trends and patterns that inform their advertising strategies.

Summary

Overall, cutting-edge analytics tools offer a powerful solution for businesses looking to stay ahead of the competition in the fast-paced world of digital advertising. By leveraging the capabilities of these tools, businesses gain a deeper understanding of their competitors, optimize their own advertising strategies, and ultimately drive better results for their bottom line.

C. Integration of AI and Machine Learning in Competitive Ad Intelligence

In digital advertising landscape, staying ahead of the competition is crucial for businesses looking to maximize their advertising efforts. One way to gain a competitive edge is through the integration of artificial intelligence (AI) and machine learning in competitive ad intelligence.

Competitive ad intelligence involves monitoring and analyzing the advertising strategies of your competitors to gain insights and improve your own campaigns. By leveraging AI and machine learning technologies, businesses take their competitive ad intelligence to the next level.

AI algorithms analyze vast amounts of data from various sources, such as social media, search engines, and websites, to provide real-time insights into competitors' ad campaigns. This piece of information helps businesses understand their competitors' targeting strategies, ad placements, and messaging, allowing them to make more informed decisions about their own advertising efforts.

Machine learning algorithms also predict the performance of different ad creatives and placements, helping businesses optimize their campaigns for maximum impact. By continuously analyzing and learning from data, machine learning algorithms adapt and improve over time, leading to more effective advertising strategies.

Summary

Overall, the integration of AI and machine learning in competitive ad intelligence give businesses a significant advantage in the crowded digital advertising space. By leveraging these technologies to gain insights into competitors' strategies and optimize their own campaigns, businesses drive better results and stay ahead of the competition.

D. The Role of Predictive Modelling in Competitive Ad Intelligence

Need to stay ahead in the competitive world of advertising, having a solid understanding of your competitors' strategies is crucial. This is where predictive modelling comes into play, providing valuable insights into the competitive ad intelligence landscape.

Competitive ad intelligence refers to the process of gathering and analyzing data on your competitors' advertising campaigns to inform your own strategies. By leveraging predictive modelling techniques, advertisers gain a deeper understanding of their competitors' tactics and make more informed decisions about their own campaigns.

One key role of predictive modelling in competitive ad intelligence is forecasting. By analyzing historical data and trends, advertisers predict future advertising strategies and outcomes. This allows them to anticipate their competitors' moves and adjust their own campaigns accordingly.

Another important aspect of predictive modelling in competitive ad intelligence is optimization. By using predictive models to analyze data on ad performance, advertisers identify areas for improvement and optimize their campaigns for better results. This helps them stay one step ahead of their competitors and drive better ROI.

Summary

Predictive modelling plays a crucial role in competitive ad intelligence by providing valuable insights into competitors' strategies, forecasting future trends, and optimizing ad campaigns for maximum impact. By incorporating predictive modelling into their advertising strategies, advertisers gain a competitive edge and achieve greater success in the ever-evolving world of digital advertising.

Section: 8. Adapting to Platform Changes in Competitive Ad Intelligence

In the ever-evolving world of digital advertising, staying ahead of the competition requires constant adaptation to platform changes. This is especially true when it comes to competitive ad intelligence, where monitoring and analyzing your competitors' advertising strategies give you a leg up in the market.

One key aspect of adapting to platform changes in competitive ad intelligence is staying up to date with the latest features and updates on the platforms you are using for advertising. For example, social media platforms like Facebook and Instagram are constantly rolling out new ad formats and targeting options, which significantly impact the effectiveness of your ad campaigns. By keeping a close eye on these changes and experimenting with new features, you stay ahead of the curve and outperform your competitors.

Another important aspect of adapting to platform changes in competitive ad intelligence is being flexible and willing to pivot your strategies when necessary. For example, if a platform changes its algorithm or ad policies, you may need to adjust your targeting or messaging to comply with the new rules. By being proactive and agile in your approach, you ensure that your ads continue to perform well and maintain a competitive edge.

In addition, it's crucial to regularly monitor your competitors' advertising efforts and analyze their strategies to identify any new trends or tactics that you can incorporate into your own campaigns. By leveraging competitive ad intelligence tools and keeping a close eye on your rivals, you stay one step ahead and continuously improve your advertising performance.

Summary

Overall, adapting to platform changes in competitive ad intelligence requires a combination of staying informed, being flexible, and actively monitoring your competitors. By staying ahead of the curve and continuously optimizing your ad campaigns, you maintain a competitive edge and drive success in the ever-changing world of digital advertising.

A. The Dynamic Nature of Advertising Platforms

The world of advertising is involving and staying ahead of the competition is crucial. With the rise of digital advertising, advertising platforms have become increasingly dynamic, offering new and innovative ways for brands to reach their target audiences. Competitive ad intelligence plays a key role in helping businesses navigate this complex landscape and stay ahead of the curve.

One of the key aspects of competitive ad intelligence is understanding the strategies and tactics that your competitors are using to promote their products or services. By analyzing their ads, messaging, and targeting techniques, you gain valuable insights into what is working in your industry and identify opportunities to differentiate your brand.

Another important aspect of competitive ad intelligence is monitoring the performance of your own ads in comparison to your competitors. By tracking metrics such as click-through rates, conversion rates, and ad placement, you identify areas where you are falling behind and make adjustments to improve your results.

In today's fast-paced digital world, advertising platforms are constantly evolving to meet the changing needs of consumers and businesses. By staying on top of these changes and leveraging competitive ad intelligence, you ensure that your brand remains competitive and relevant in the ever-changing advertising landscape.

B. Strategies for Adapting to Algorithm Updates

In the evolving world of digital advertising, staying on top of algorithm updates is crucial for maintaining a competitive edge. With search engines like Google constantly tweaking their algorithms to provide users with the most relevant and high-quality content, it's important for businesses to adapt their strategies accordingly. Here are some key strategies for staying ahead of the game when it comes to algorithm updates:

1. Stay Informed: Keeping up-to-date with the latest algorithm updates is key to adapting your strategies effectively. Subscribe to industry newsletters, follow reputable digital marketing blogs, and attend webinars to stay informed about any changes that may impact your online presence.

2. Monitor Your Competition: Utilizing competitive ad intelligence tools help you stay ahead of the competition by providing insights into their ad strategies, keywords, and performance. By analyzing what is working for your competitors, you adapt your own strategies to stay competitive in the ever-changing digital landscape.

3. Focus on Quality Content: With search engines placing a greater emphasis on high-quality, relevant content, it's important to prioritize creating valuable content that resonates with your target audience. By focusing on quality over quantity, you improve your chances of ranking well in search engine results pages.

4. Diversify Your Advertising Channels: In light of algorithm updates that may impact your organic search rankings, it's important to diversify your advertising channels. Investing in paid search advertising and social media advertising help you maintain a strong online presence.

5. Test and Iterate: As algorithms continue to evolve, it's important to continuously test and iterate on your strategies to see what works best for your business. By monitoring key performance indicators and adjusting your tactics accordingly, you stay ahead of the curve and adapt to algorithm updates effectively.

By staying informed, monitoring your competition, focusing on quality content, diversifying your marketing channels, and testing and iterating on your strategies, you adapt to algorithm updates and maintain a competitive edge in the digital marketing landscape.

C. Case Studies of Successful Adaptation

In the world of advertising, staying ahead of the competition is crucial for success. One way that companies gain an edge is through utilizing competitive ad intelligence. By studying the strategies and tactics of their competitors, businesses adapt and improve their own advertising efforts to drive better results.

Case studies of successful adaptation provide valuable insights into how companies have used competitive ad intelligence to their advantage. By examining real-world examples, we learn from their experiences and apply similar strategies to our own campaigns.

One such case study is that of a leading tech company that used competitive ad intelligence to identify gaps in their competitor's advertising strategy. By analyzing the keywords and messaging used in their competitor's ads, the company was able to create more targeted and effective campaigns that resonated with their target audience.

Another example is a popular e-commerce brand that used competitive ad intelligence to optimize its digital advertising spend. By monitoring its competitor's ad placements and performance metrics, the brand was able to reallocate its budget to focus on channels that were driving the best results.

In both cases, these companies were able to adapt and improve their advertising strategies by leveraging competitive ad intelligence. By staying informed about what their competitors were doing, they were able to make data-driven decisions that led to increased brand visibility, engagement, and ultimately, sales.

Summary

Case studies of successful adaptation demonstrate the power of competitive ad intelligence in helping companies stay ahead of the competition. By learning from the experiences of others and applying similar strategies to our own campaigns, they experienced better results and achieved their advertising goals.

Section: 9. Leveraging Emerging Technologies of Blockchain and, Virtual and Augmented Reality

In today's rapidly evolving digital landscape, businesses are constantly seeking innovative ways to stay ahead of the competition. One of the key strategies to achieve this is by leveraging emerging technologies such as blockchain, virtual reality (VR), and augmented reality (AR). These cutting-edge technologies have the potential to revolutionize the way businesses operate, interact with customers, and drive growth.

Blockchain technology, often associated with cryptocurrencies like Bitcoin, is a decentralized and secured way of recording transactions. By utilizing blockchain, businesses ensure transparency, security, and efficiency in their operations. This leads to cost savings, improved trust among stakeholders, and streamlined processes.

Virtual and augmented reality, on the other hand, offer immersive and interactive experiences for users. VR technology allows users to enter a completely virtual world, while AR overlays digital information onto the real world. Businesses leverage these technologies to create engaging advertising campaigns, enhance customer experiences, and even improve employee training programs.

By incorporating blockchain, VR, and AR into their operations, businesses gain a competitive edge in their industry. However, in order to effectively implement these technologies, it is crucial to conduct thorough competitive ad intelligence research. This involves analyzing the strategies and tactics of competitors in the market, identifying key trends and opportunities, and developing a comprehensive plan to leverage blockchain, VR, and AR effectively.

Summary

The integration of blockchain, virtual reality, and augmented reality technologies provide businesses with a significant advantage in today's competitive landscape. By staying ahead of the curve and harnessing the power of these emerging technologies, businesses drive innovation, improve customer engagement, and ultimately achieve long-term success.

A. Blockchain Technology

Blockchain technology has been hailed as a transformative force across various industries, and its impact on the digital advertising landscape is no exception. Digital advertising suffers from several issues including ad fraud, lack of transparency, inefficiency, and disputes over metrics. Blockchain offers potential solutions to these problems by providing a decentralized, transparent, and immutable ledger system.

One of the key benefits of blockchain in digital advertising is transparency. The technology allows for the creation of a decentralized ledger that records every transaction or interaction in the advertising supply chain. This transparency helps to combat issues such as ad fraud and ensures that advertisers get what they pay for.

Ad fraud is a significant concern in digital advertising, with estimates suggesting that billions of dollars are lost to fraudulent activities each year. Blockchain helps mitigate ad fraud by providing a secure and transparent system for tracking ad impressions, clicks, and conversions.

Furthermore, blockchain technology improves the targeting and personalization of ads while still protecting user privacy. By securely storing user data on the blockchain, advertisers access valuable insights without compromising individual privacy. This approach empowers users to have greater control over their data and ensures that advertisers are targeting the right audience with their ads.

Another area where blockchain revolutionizes digital advertising is in micropayments and content monetization. With blockchain-based micropayment systems, content creators are directly compensated for their work without the need for intermediaries. This opens up new revenue streams for publishers and incentivizes quality content creation.

However, despite its potential, blockchain technology is still in its infancy in the digital advertising space. Implementation challenges, scalability issues, and regulatory concerns need to be addressed before blockchain realizes its full potential in revolutionizing the digital advertising landscape.

Overall, blockchain has the potential to transform the digital advertising industry by providing transparency, combating ad fraud, improving targeting and personalization, and enabling new revenue models. As the technology continues to mature, we expect to see more widespread adoption and innovative use cases emerge in the digital advertising space.

B. The Impact of Blockchain on Competitive Ad Intelligence

In the world of digital advertising, transparency has always been a hot topic. With the rise of blockchain technology, the advertising industry is now seeing a major shift towards increased transparency and accountability. Blockchain, a decentralized and secure ledger system, has the potential to revolutionize the way ads are bought, sold, and tracked online.

One of the key areas where blockchain is making a significant impact is in competitive ad intelligence. This refers to the ability for advertisers to gain insights into their competitors' advertising strategies, placements, and performance metrics. By leveraging blockchain technology, advertisers access real-time data on their competitors' ads, allowing them to make more informed decisions about their own advertising campaigns.

Blockchain also offers a level of transparency that is unparalleled in the advertising industry. With traditional advertising methods, there is often a lack of visibility into how ad placements are being purchased and whether the data being used is accurate. Blockchain technology, on the other hand, provides a secure and transparent way for advertisers to track the journey of their ads from creation to placement, ensuring that every impression is accounted for.

Furthermore, blockchain helps combat issues such as ad fraud and click fraud, which have long plagued the digital advertising industry. By using blockchain to verify the authenticity of ad placements and track the flow of ad dollars, advertisers reduce the risk of fraudulent activity and ensure that their campaigns are reaching their intended audience.

Summary

Blockchain technology is set to have a profound impact on ad transparency in the digital advertising industry. By providing advertisers with real-time competitive ad intelligence and a secure, transparent way to track their ad placements, blockchain is revolutionizing the way ads are bought, sold, and monitored online. As the technology continues to evolve, we expect to see even greater levels of transparency and accountability in the world of digital advertising.

C. Virtual and Augmented Reality Technology

Virtual and augmented reality (VR and AR) are revolutionizing the digital advertising landscape in several significant ways:

Immersive Brand Experiences: VR and AR allow advertisers to create immersive brand experiences that engage users on a deeper level. Instead of traditional advertising formats, users interact with products or services in a virtual environment, leading to increased brand awareness and customer engagement.

Personalized Advertising: VR and AR technologies enable advertisers to deliver highly personalized advertising experiences based on user preferences and behavior. By collecting data on user interactions within virtual environments, advertisers tailor ads to individual interests, enhancing relevance and effectiveness.

Enhanced Storytelling: VR and AR provide new opportunities for advertisers to tell compelling stories and convey brand messages in innovative ways. Advertisers create immersive narratives that captivate audiences and leave a lasting impression, leading to increased brand loyalty and advocacy.

Interactive Product Demonstrations: VR and AR allow advertisers to showcase products and services through interactive demonstrations that simulate real-world experiences. Users virtually try on clothing, test drive cars, or explore destinations, leading to more informed purchasing decisions and higher conversion rates.

Location-Based Advertising: AR technology enables location-based advertising experiences that overlay digital content onto the physical world. Advertisers deliver targeted ads based on a user's location, allowing for highly relevant and contextualized messaging that drives foot traffic and sales.

Social Sharing and Virality: VR and AR experiences are inherently shareable, making them ideal for social media platforms. Users easily share their virtual experiences with friends and followers, leading to increased brand visibility and virality.

Measurable ROI: VR and AR advertising campaigns offer robust analytics and measurement capabilities, allowing advertisers to track user engagement, interactions, and conversions in real-time. The data-driven approach enables advertisers to optimize campaigns for maximum ROI and effectiveness.

Overall, VR and AR technologies are transforming the digital advertising landscape by offering immersive, personalized, and interactive experiences that capture audience attention and drive results. As these technologies continue to evolve, advertisers must adapt their strategies to leverage the full potential of VR and AR in reaching and engaging consumers.

D. The Impact of Virtual and Augmented Reality on Competitive Ad Intelligence

In today's digital age, advertisers are constantly looking for innovative ways to capture the attention of their target audience. One of the most exciting developments in recent years has been the use of virtual and augmented reality in competitive ad intelligence. These technologies have the ability to create immersive and interactive experiences that engage consumers in ways that traditional advertising simply cannot.

One of the key benefits of using virtual and augmented reality in competitive ad intelligence is the ability to create truly memorable experiences for consumers. By allowing them to interact with a brand in a virtual environment, advertisers forge a deeper connection with their audience and leave a lasting impression. This leads to increased brand loyalty and ultimately, higher sales.

Another advantage of virtual and augmented reality advertising is the ability to target specific audience segments with personalized content. By collecting data on consumer preferences and behaviors, advertisers create custom experiences that resonate with their target demographic. This leads to higher engagement rates and a greater return on investment.

However, it's important to remember that virtual and augmented reality advertising is still a relatively new and evolving field. As such, advertisers need to be willing to experiment and adapt their strategies in order to stay ahead of the curve. By leveraging competitive ad intelligence and staying up-to-date on the latest trends, advertisers ensure that their virtual and augmented reality ad campaigns are as effective as possible.

Summary

Virtual and augmented reality have the potential to revolutionize the world of digital advertising. By creating immersive and interactive experiences, advertisers engage consumers in ways that were previously unimaginable. By utilizing competitive ad intelligence and staying on top of the latest trends, advertisers ensure that their virtual and augmented reality ad campaigns are a success.

Section: 10. Ethical Considerations in Competitive Ad Intelligence

In the competitive world of advertising, companies are constantly seeking ways to gain an edge over their rivals. One tactic that has become increasingly popular is competitive ad intelligence, which involves analyzing the advertising strategies of competitors to gain insights and inform one's own advertising strategy. While this practice provides valuable information, it also raises a number of ethical considerations that must be taken into account.

One of the primary ethical considerations in competitive ad intelligence is the issue of privacy. When analyzing the advertising strategies of competitors, companies inadvertently access sensitive information about their rivals, such as their advertising strategies, target demographics, and future plans. This raises questions about the ethical implications of using this piece of information to gain a competitive advantage, as it may be obtained without the consent of the competitor.

Another ethical consideration is the potential for misinformation or manipulation. In the fast-paced world of advertising, companies are tempted to use competitive ad intelligence to spread false or misleading information about their competitors in order to gain an advantage. This raises questions about the ethical implications of using deceptive tactics to undermine competitors and deceive consumers.

Additionally, there is the issue of intellectual property rights. When analyzing the advertising strategies of competitors, companies must be careful not to infringe on their intellectual property rights, such as trademarks, copyrights, or patents. Using competitive ad intelligence to copy or imitate the creative work of competitors without permission may lead to legal consequences and damage to the company's reputation.

Summary

While competitive ad intelligence provides valuable insights and inform advertising strategies, it is important for companies to consider the ethical implications of this practice. By respecting the privacy of competitors, avoiding misinformation and manipulation, and respecting intellectual property rights, companies ensure that their use of competitive ad intelligence is ethical and responsible.

A. Privacy Concerns

In today's digital age, privacy concerns have become a hot topic of discussion. With the rise of competitive ad intelligence tools, many individuals are becoming increasingly worried about the amount of personal information being collected and used by companies for targeted advertising.

One major concern with competitive ad intelligence is the potential invasion of privacy. These tools allow companies to track and monitor their competitors' advertising strategies, which often involves collecting data on consumers' online behavior. This includes everything from the websites they visit to the products they purchase, creating a detailed profile of individuals without their knowledge or consent.

Another issue is the lack of transparency surrounding how the data are used. While companies claim that they are using competitive ad intelligence for marketing purposes, there is often little information provided about how exactly this piece of information is used and shared. This lack of transparency leaves consumers feeling uneasy about the security of their personal information.

Additionally, the use of competitive ad intelligence leads to an increase in targeted advertising. Seeing ads for products they have recently searched for or discussed make people feel like their every move is being watched and analyzed, leading to a loss of trust in the companies collecting the data.

Overall, privacy concerns surrounding competitive ad intelligence are a growing issue in today's digital landscape. As technology continues to advance, it is important for companies to prioritize transparency and consumer trust when it comes to collecting and using personal data for advertising purposes. By addressing these concerns and taking steps to protect consumer privacy, companies build stronger relationships with their customers and avoid potential backlash in the future.

B. Responsible Data Usage

In today's digital age, data have become valuable commodity that companies use to gain insights into consumer behavior and preferences. However, with great power comes great responsibility, and it is crucial for businesses to use data ethically and responsibly.

One area where responsible data usage is particularly important is in competitive ad intelligence. This practice involves analyzing the advertising strategies of competitors to gain a competitive edge in the market. While this is a valuable tool for businesses looking to stay ahead of the competition, it is important to approach competitive ad intelligence with caution and respect for consumer privacy.

One key aspect of responsible data usage in competitive ad intelligence is ensuring that data is collected and analyzed in a legal and ethical manner. This means obtaining consent from consumers before collecting their data and ensuring that data collected are anonymized and used solely for the purpose of analyzing advertising strategies.

Another important consideration is the security of the data being used for competitive ad intelligence. Businesses must take steps to protect the data they collect from competitors and ensure that they are not vulnerable to cyberattacks or data breaches.

Additionally, businesses must be transparent with consumers about how their data are used for competitive ad intelligence. This means clearly communicating with consumers about the types of data collected and how they will be used, as well as giving consumers the option to opt out of having their data used for this purpose.

Summary

Responsible data usage is essential in all aspects of business, including competitive ad intelligence. By approaching data collection and analysis with caution, respect for consumer privacy, and transparency, businesses gain valuable insights from competitive ad intelligence while also maintaining the trust of their customers.

C. Regulatory Compliance

In the world of digital advertising, staying compliant with regulations is crucial for businesses looking to gain a competitive edge. Regulatory compliance in the realm of competitive ad intelligence ensures that companies are following the rules and guidelines set forth by governing bodies to avoid fines and penalties.

One of the key aspects of regulatory compliance in competitive ad intelligence is ensuring that ads are not misleading or deceptive. Companies must adhere to strict advertising standards to ensure that their messaging is truthful and accurate. This includes providing clear disclosures about products or services advertised and avoiding false or exaggerated claims.

Another important aspect of regulatory compliance in competitive ad intelligence is protecting consumer privacy. With the rise of data-driven advertising, companies must be diligent in safeguarding personal information collected from users. This includes obtaining proper consent for data collection and storage, as well as implementing security measures to prevent data breaches.

Additionally, companies must also comply with industry-specific regulations that govern advertising practices. For example, pharmaceutical companies must adhere to strict guidelines when promoting prescription drugs, while financial institutions must follow regulations set by agencies like the SEC and FINRA.

Overall, regulatory compliance in competitive ad intelligence is essential for companies looking to maintain a positive reputation and stay in good standing with regulators. By following best practices and staying up-to-date on the latest regulations, businesses ensure that their advertising efforts are effective, ethical, and compliant.

Section: 11. Strategic Implementation of Competitive Ad Intelligence

In today's competitive business landscape, staying ahead of the competition is crucial for success. One way to gain a competitive edge is through the strategic implementation of competitive ad intelligence. There two roads to access and follow. These are assessing current analytics practices and the strategic option.

A. Current Analytics Practices

Having a strong understanding of current analytics practices is crucial. By assessing the way your competitors are utilizing analytics tools and strategies, you gain valuable insights that help inform and improve your own advertising efforts. Competitive ad intelligence is a key component of assessing current analytics practices. By analyzing the advertising strategies of your competitors, you gain a better understanding of how they are reaching their target audience, which platforms they are using, and what messaging is resonating with consumers. This piece of information helps you identify gaps in your own advertising strategy and make adjustments to better compete in the market.

One way to gather competitive ad intelligence is through the use of analytics tools such as SEMrush or SpyFu. These tools provide you with valuable data on your competitors' ad spend, keyword rankings, and ad performance metrics. By analyzing the data, you gain a better understanding of what is working for your competitors and how to adapt your own advertising strategy to better compete.

In addition to using analytics tools, it is also important to conduct manual research on your competitors' advertising practices. This involves monitoring their social media accounts, websites, and other digital channels to see what types of ads they are running and how they are engaging with their audience. By staying up-to-date on your competitors' advertising efforts, you ensure that your own advertising strategy remains competitive and relevant.

Summary

Assessing current analytics practices, particularly in the realm of competitive ad intelligence, is essential for staying ahead in the competitive landscape of digital advertising. By leveraging analytics tools and conducting manual research on your competitors, you gain valuable insights that inform and improve your own advertising strategy. By staying informed and proactive in your approach to analytics, you position your brand for success in the ever-evolving digital advertising landscape.

B. Strategic Option

By analyzing the advertising strategies of competitors, businesses uncover valuable insights that inform their own strategic options. First, identify gaps in the market. By analyzing the advertising tactics of competitors, businesses identify areas where competitors are neglecting to target. This presents an opportunity for businesses to fill these gaps and target new audience segments that have been overlooked by competitors.

Another strategic option that businesses consider is to differentiate their advertising messaging. By analyzing the ad copy, visuals, and overall messaging of competitors, businesses identify common themes and messaging strategies that are used within their industry. By taking a different approach and offering a unique value proposition, businesses set themselves apart from the competition and attract a new audience.

Additionally, competitive ad intelligence also helps businesses optimize their advertising spend. By analyzing the ad placements, frequency, and messaging of competitors, businesses identify which advertising channels are most effective for reaching their target audience. This helps businesses allocate their advertising budget more efficiently and maximize their return on investment.

Summary

Competitive ad intelligence is a valuable tool that businesses use to inform their strategic options. By analyzing the advertising strategies of competitors, businesses uncover new opportunities, differentiate their messaging, and optimize their advertising spend. By leveraging competitive ad intelligence, businesses stay ahead of the competition and achieve long-term success in the marketplace.

C. Integrating Competitive Ad Intelligence into Existing Workflows

Competitive ad intelligence is a powerful tool that provides valuable insights into the advertising strategies of your rivals, allowing you to make informed decisions about your own campaigns.

Integrating competitive ad intelligence into your existing workflows helps you streamline your advertising efforts and maximize your ROI. By closely monitoring the ads of your competitors, you identify trends, uncover new opportunities, and optimize your own campaigns for better results.

One key benefit of integrating competitive ad intelligence into your workflows is the ability to track changes in your competitors' strategies in real-time. By keeping a close eye on their ads, you quickly adapt your own campaigns to stay ahead of the curve and capitalize on emerging trends.

Additionally, competitive ad intelligence helps you identify gaps in the market that your competitors may be missing. By analyzing their ad placements, messaging, and targeting strategies, you uncover new opportunities to reach your target audience and drive more conversions.

To effectively integrate competitive ad intelligence into your existing workflows, consider using a dedicated tool or platform that provides comprehensive insights into your competitors' advertising activities. Look for features such as ad monitoring, keyword tracking, and performance analytics to gain a complete picture of the competitive landscape.

Summary

Integrating competitive ad intelligence into your existing workflows gives you a competitive advantage in the crowded digital advertising space. By leveraging this valuable tool, you stay one step ahead of your competitors, optimize your campaigns for better results, and ultimately drive more success for your business.

Section: 12. Case Studies of Successful Implementations of Competitive Ad Intelligence

In this segment I will delve into case studies of successful implementations of competitive ad intelligence. Competitive ad intelligence refers to the process of analyzing and understanding the advertising strategies and tactics of your competitors in order to gain a competitive edge in the market.

Case Study 1: Company A

Company A, a leading e-commerce retailer, wanted to increase their market share and improve their advertising ROI. By utilizing competitive ad intelligence tools, the retailer was able to track its competitors' ad placements, messaging, and targeting strategies. This allowed it to identify gaps in the market and tailor its own advertising campaigns to better resonate with its target audience. As a result, company A saw a significant increase in website traffic and sales, ultimately surpassing their competitors in the market.

Case Study 2: Company B

Company B, a software company, was struggling to differentiate themselves in a crowded market. Through competitive ad intelligence, the company was able to identify key messaging and positioning strategies that their competitors were using successfully. By leveraging this piece of information, Company B was able to revamp their own advertising campaigns and highlight its unique selling points. This resulted in a noticeable increase in brand awareness and lead generation, ultimately helping it to stand out in the market.

These case studies highlighted the importance of utilizing competitive ad intelligence to inform and optimize your advertising strategies. By understanding your competitors' tactics and leveraging this piece of information to your advantage, you drive better results and outperform the competition.

Section 13. The Future Trends in Competitive Ad Intelligence

In the ever-evolving world of digital advertising, staying ahead of the competition is crucial. One way to do this is by utilizing competitive ad intelligence tools to gain insights into what your competitors are doing and how you outperform them. In this segment I will discuss the future trends in competitive ad intelligence and how they help you stay ahead in the game.

1. AI-Powered Insights:

One of the biggest trends in competitive ad intelligence is the use of artificial intelligence to analyze and interpret data. AI-powered tools help you uncover patterns and trends in your competitors' ad strategies, allowing you to make more informed decisions about your own campaigns. By leveraging AI, you gain a competitive edge and stay one step ahead of the competition.

2. Cross-Channel Analysis:

Another trend in competitive ad intelligence is the focus on cross-channel analysis. In today's digital landscape, consumers interact with brands across multiple channels, from social media to search engines to email. By analyzing your competitors' ad strategies across all these channels, you better understand their overall marketing approach and identify opportunities to differentiate yourself.

3. Real-Time Monitoring:

As the digital advertising landscape continues to evolve rapidly, real-time monitoring of your competitors' ad campaigns is becoming increasingly important. By staying up-to-date on your competitors' latest moves, you quickly adjust your own strategies to stay competitive. Real-time monitoring tools help you track your competitors' ad performance, keywords, and messaging, allowing you to make timely adjustments to your own campaigns.

4. Personalization and Customization:

In the future, competitive ad intelligence tools will likely focus more on personalization and customization. By analyzing your competitors' ad targeting and messaging strategies, you tailor your own campaigns to better resonate with your target audience. Personalization and customization help you stand out in a crowded marketplace and drive better results for your business.

Summary

Competitive ad intelligence is a powerful tool for staying ahead of the competition in the digital advertising landscape. By leveraging AI-powered insights, cross-channel analysis, real-time monitoring, and personalization, you gain a competitive edge and drive better results for your business.

A. Shifting Consumer Behaviors in Competitive Ad Intelligence

Consumer behavior is constantly evolving, especially in today's competitive market where brands are constantly vying for attention. One key tool that companies use to stay ahead of the game is competitive ad intelligence. By monitoring and analyzing the advertising strategies of their competitors, businesses gain valuable insights into shifting consumer behaviors and tailor their own marketing efforts accordingly.

One important aspect of competitive ad intelligence is understanding how consumers are interacting with different types of ads. Are they more responsive to traditional print ads, or do they prefer interactive digital ads? By studying the ad campaigns of competitors, companies gain a better understanding of which tactics are most effective in capturing consumer attention.

Another key factor in shifting consumer behaviors is the rise of social media and influencer marketing. Consumers are increasingly turning to social media platforms like Instagram and TikTok for product recommendations and inspiration. By keeping a close eye on how competitors are leveraging social media influencers in their ad campaigns, businesses adapt their own strategies to better connect with their target audience.

Additionally, the shift towards online shopping has also had a significant impact on consumer behaviors. With more and more consumers turning to e-commerce platforms for their shopping needs, businesses need to ensure that their online ads are optimized for maximum visibility and engagement. By analyzing the ad placement and messaging of competitors in the online space, companies stay ahead of the curve and effectively reach their target audience.

Summary

Competitive ad intelligence is a crucial tool for businesses looking to stay ahead in today's constantly evolving market. By monitoring and analyzing the advertising strategies of competitors, companies gain valuable insights into shifting consumer behaviors and adapt their own marketing efforts accordingly. By staying proactive and keeping a close eye on industry trends, businesses position themselves for success in the ever-changing world of consumer behavior.

B. Moving Beyond Traditional Analytics

In today's rapidly evolving digital landscape, traditional analytics alone may not be enough to stay ahead of the competition. With the rise of online advertising and the increasing complexity of consumer behavior, businesses need to move beyond traditional analytics to gain a competitive edge.

One powerful tool that helps businesses stay ahead of the curve is competitive ad intelligence. By analyzing the advertising strategies of competitors, businesses gain valuable insights into their own industry, target audience, and potential opportunities for growth.

Competitive ad intelligence allows businesses to track the performance of their competitors' ads, identify trends in their advertising strategies, and even uncover new advertising channels that may be worth exploring. By understanding what is working for their competitors and what isn't, businesses make more informed decisions about their own advertising campaigns.

In addition to analyzing competitors' ads, competitive ad intelligence also helps businesses identify emerging trends in their industry, monitor changes in consumer behavior, and stay up-to-date on the latest advertising tactics. By staying ahead of the curve, businesses position themselves as industry leaders and capture a larger share of the market.

Overall, moving beyond traditional analytics and incorporating competitive ad intelligence into your advertising strategy give your business a competitive edge in today's fast-paced digital world. By staying informed, adapting to changing trends, and learning from your competitors, you drive better results and achieve long-term success.

C. Ongoing Learning in Staying Ahead in the Dynamic Advertising Landscape

In today's fast-paced advertising landscape, staying ahead of the competition requires ongoing learning and adaptation. With the rise of digital advertising and the ever-evolving consumer preferences, it is crucial for advertisers to constantly stay informed about the latest trends and strategies in order to effectively reach their target audience.

One key aspect of staying ahead in the dynamic advertising landscape is utilizing competitive ad intelligence. This involves analyzing the advertising strategies of your competitors to gain insights into what is working well and what could be improved upon. By monitoring the ads of your competitors, you identify new trends, creative approaches, and messaging strategies that resonate with your target audience.

Competitive ad intelligence also helps you identify gaps in the market that your competitors may have overlooked. By understanding what your competitors are doing, you better position your own advertising campaigns to stand out and capture the attention of potential customers.

In addition, ongoing learning through competitive ad intelligence allows advertisers to stay up-to-date on industry changes and emerging technologies. By constantly monitoring the advertising landscape, you adapt your strategies to take advantage of new opportunities and stay ahead of the curve.

Overall, ongoing learning and utilizing competitive ad intelligence are essential components of staying ahead in the dynamic advertising landscape. By staying informed, analyzing your competitors, and adapting your strategies accordingly, you ensure that your advertising campaigns remain effective and relevant in an ever-changing market.

Section: 14. Recap of Key Concepts in Competitive Ad Intelligence

In this section, I will do a recap of key concepts in competitive ad intelligence. Competitive ad intelligence is a crucial aspect of any advertising strategy, as it allows businesses to gain insights into their competitors' advertising tactics and performance. By analyzing competitors' ads, businesses identify trends, uncover new strategies, and ultimately improve their own advertising efforts.

One key concept in competitive ad intelligence is ad monitoring. This involves keeping track of competitors' ads across various channels, such as social media, search engines, and display networks. By monitoring competitors' ads, businesses stay up-to-date on their messaging, creative elements, and targeting strategies.

Another important concept is ad analysis. This involves analyzing competitors' ads to understand their messaging, positioning, and calls-to-action. By dissecting competitors' ads, businesses identify strengths and weaknesses in their own advertising efforts and make informed decisions on how to improve.

Competitive benchmarking is also a key concept in competitive ad intelligence. This involves comparing your own ad performance to that of competitors to gauge your market position. By benchmarking against competitors, businesses identify areas for improvement and set realistic goals for their advertising campaigns.

Overall, competitive ad intelligence is a valuable tool for businesses looking to stay ahead of the competition. By monitoring competitors' ads, analyzing their strategies, and benchmarking against them, businesses gain valuable insights and make informed decisions to improve their advertising efforts.

A. Glossary of Terms

When diving into the world of competitive ad intelligence, it's important to familiarize yourself with the glossary of terms that are commonly used in the industry. Understanding these terms will not only help you navigate through the vast amount of data available, but also allow you to make more informed decisions when it comes to your advertising strategies.

Here are some key terms to keep in mind:

1. Ad Impressions: The number of times an ad is displayed to a user.

2. Click-through Rate (CTR): The percentage of people who click on an ad after seeing it.

3. Cost Per Click (CPC): The amount of money paid for each click on an ad.

4. Conversion Rate: The percentage of people who take a desired action after clicking on an ad.

5. Ad Placement: Where an ad is displayed on a webpage or app.

6. Ad Creative: The visual and text components of an ad.

7. Ad Copy: The written content of an ad.

8. Ad Network: A platform that connects advertisers with publishers to display ads.

By understanding these terms and how they relate to competitive ad intelligence, you better analyze and optimize your advertising campaigns.

Section 15 Resources

In the world of digital advertising, having access to competitive ad intelligence resources is crucial for staying ahead of the game. These resources provide valuable insights into what your competitors are doing in terms of their advertising strategies, allowing you to make more informed decisions about your own campaigns.

One key resource for competitive ad intelligence is a tool that allows you to monitor your competitors' ad placements across various platforms. By keeping track of where your competitors are advertising, you identify new opportunities for reaching your target audience and potentially outmaneuvering your competition.

Another important resource is the database of ad creatives, which allows you to see the actual ads that your competitors are running including social proof. This gives you a better understanding of their messaging and creative strategies, helping you to craft more effective ads of your own.

Additionally, tools that provide insights into your competitors' ad performance metrics, such as click-through rates and conversion rates, help you gauge the effectiveness of your own campaigns and make data-driven optimizations.

Summary

Having access to competitive ad intelligence resources is essential for staying competitive in the crowded digital advertising space. By leveraging these tools, you gain valuable insights into your competitors' strategies and make more informed decisions about your own campaigns.

A. Performance Index

When it comes to competitive ad intelligence, one of the most important tools at your disposal is the performance index. Understanding how your brand or product compares to others in your industry gives you a leg up in the world of advertising.

Performance index is a measurement that compares your brand's performance to that of your competitors. It helps you identify areas where you are excelling and where you may need to improve. By analyzing the performance index, you gain insights into what is working well for your competitors and how to adapt your own advertising strategy to stay ahead.

One key aspect of the performance index is understanding your brand's share of voice. This metric measures how much of the conversation in your industry is centered around your brand compared to your competitors. By tracking your share of voice, you see if your advertising efforts are paying off and if you are effectively reaching your target audience.

Another important factor to consider when analyzing the performance index is your brand's share of market. This metric measures how much of the market share your brand holds compared to your competitors. By understanding your share of market, you see if your advertising efforts are translating into actual sales and market dominance.

Overall, performance index is a valuable tool in competitive ad intelligence that helps you stay ahead of the curve in the ever-evolving world of advertising. By understanding how your brand stacks up against the competition, you make informed decisions about your advertising strategy and ultimately drive success for your brand.

Section 16 About the Author

Mr. Adebola Adeola, MBA (Leicester) UK ◆M.CAM, RPA, MNIPR

✨ Business Management Strategist | Digital Marketing Maestro | Advertising and Public Relations Virtuoso ✨

◆ About Me ◆

I am a seasoned Business Management professional with comprehensive knowledge in strategic planning and implementation. My rich experience, coupled with a relentless passion for excellence, has consistently driven the transformative growth of the companies I've had the privilege to serve. My expertise extends to Digital Marketing, Advertising, and Public Relations where I have orchestrated campaigns that have changed customer behaviors and driven remarkable conversions.

◆ Current Role ◆

☑ As the CEO the driving force behind Dinet Comms, a distinguished Advertising Strategy Agency, I am at the helm of a team of experts dedicated to boosting brand visibility and generating high-quality leads. Dinet Comms specializes in crafting creative strategies, content creation, programmatic advertising, and competitive advertising intelligence. email sequencing, and social media marketing, all customized to meet the unique needs of our clients.

🎯 Our Mission: To amplify your message, engage your target audience, and deliver meaningful results. 🎯 ◆ Our Extended Services ◆

💼 Financial PR Agency: https://pr.compaipa.com; 🌐 Full-Service Advertising Solutions Agency: https://compaipa.com; Content Writing and Copywriting https://ccw.compaipa.com; SEM Marketing (SEO & PPC) digitma.compaipa.com; Social Media Marketing https://somima.compaipa.com; WptApps Website Design https://wptapps.com 🖥 Outdoor Advertising Agency Solutions: https://dooh.compaipa.com; Designs CompaiPA, Creative Design Agency https://design.compaipa.com; UpBlog CompaiPA, SEO Blog Writing Services Agency https://upblog.compaipa.com, Lead CompaiPA, Generation Strategy for B2B Agency, https://lead.compaipa.com

Wrap Up

"Beyond Analytics: Unlocking the Hidden Power of Competitive Ad Intelligence" by Mr. Adebola Adeola

Unlock the secrets behind the most successful advertising strategies with "Beyond Analytics: Unlocking the Hidden Power of Competitive Ad Intelligence," authored by the brilliant Mr. Adebola Adeola, the CEO of Dinet Comms. With a wealth of experience on both the agency and client sides, Mr. Adeola brings a unique perspective on how to harness the power of competitive ad intelligence to stay ahead in today's dynamic market This insightful book is not just a read; it's an opportunity to revolutionize your approach to advertising strategy.

Leveraging his extensive educational background, including an MBA from the University of Leicester, UK, and professional certifications like M.CAM, RPA, and MNIPR, Mr. Adeola delves deep into the nuances of Competitive ad intelligence, offering practical, actionable insights that transform your brand's competitive edge. Don't miss your chance to gain insider knowledge from an industry leader. Secure your copy of "Beyond Analytics" on Amazon and take the first step toward mastering the art of competitive advertising intelligence.

◈ Let's Connect ◈

I am always open to exciting collaborations and networking opportunities in Digital Marketing Services. Feel free to connect with me and explore how we can create transformative success together.

#DigitalMarketing #Advertising #FinancialPR #Content Marketing

www.ingramcontent.com/pod-product-compliance
Lightning Source LLC
Chambersburg PA
CBHW062117220526
45471CB00010B/3766